Speak it into Existence

by

Sesvalah
with Naleighna Kai

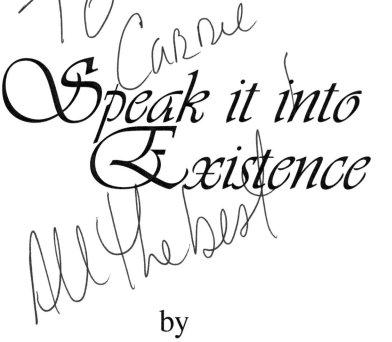

Macro Publishing Group
Chicago, Illinois
www.macropublishing.com

Copyright © 2006

A Macro Publishing Group book published by
arrangement with Sesvalah and Naleighna Kai

All rights reserved. Printed and bound in the United States of America.
No part of this book may be reproduced or utilized in any form or by
any means, electronic or mechanical, including photocopying,
recording, or by any information storage or retrieval system, except
by a reviewer who may quote brief passages in a review to be printed
in a magazine or newspaper, without permission in writing from the
Publisher. Inquiries should be addressed to the Macro Publishing
Group, Permissions Department, 16781 Torrence Avenue, # 103,
Lansing, IL 60438. Printed May 2006.

This book is designed to provide information in regards to the subject
matter covered. It is sold with the understanding that the publisher
and the authors are not engaged in rendering legal, accounting,
psychological or other professional services. If advice or other expert
services are required, the services of a professional of your choosing
should be sought. While every attempt has been made to provide
accurate information, neither the authors nor the publisher can be
held accountable for any error or omission.

Any slights of people, places, belief systems or organizations are
unintentional.

ISBN (10):   0-9754130-3-1
ISBN (13): 9780975413036
LCCN: 2006926525

Edited by Marilyn Weishaar (www.theweisrevise.com),
Christine Meister and Lissa Woodson (www.macropublishing.com)
Cover design by Barron Steward (www.barronsteward.com)
Interior design by Lissa Woodson

Sesvalah's Acknowledgments:

I would like to first give honor to God, the Creator, who is the head of my life, in whom I move and have my being. I would also like to thank three spiritual teachers. First, my wonderful insightful mother, Clara Jones, who has made her transition. She was my first teacher and taught me about love, God, and that there was so much more to life than what we could see with the physical eyes.

Second, the Rev. Mary M. Mays, a powerful healer, teacher, and bold metaphysician, who has also made her transition. She introduced me to the principle of oneness, that we must be accountable for our actions and to be aware of the motives behind our actions.

Then there is the unorthodox Rev. Joan Lopez-Roberts, who is an exceptionally intuitive healer, teacher, and preacher who has, and continues to, expand my knowledge about the spirit world, the love that God has for us, and so many other things.

I would also like to thank my husband, Tehuti, who always encourages and supports me in whatever path I decide to walk. My two wonderful children, André and Leslie, whose constant support, encouragement and witty comments remind me to "stay on the path" and to "practice what I preach." They keep me grounded in love and in practicing being nonjudgmental.

I would also like to thank my assistant minister and friend, Earlee Hubbard, who is always ready to step in and assist me in whatever needs to be done.

To all the members of Prayer, Praise and Faith Ministries.

To Lissa, who is like a bulldog who will not let go when she has something in her clutches, I thank you for refusing to let me stop.

I thank my sisters and brother whom I love dearly, and from whom I constantly learn about life and myself. And last, but certainly not least, I thank all of the ancestors on whose shoulders we stand and all of the members of the angelic kingdom who God has sent to assist us as we continue to journey on this path called life.

Wishing you peace and love light and joy,

Sesvalah

This book is dedicated to the light we know and love as:
ANDRE GILMER

Naleighna Kai's Acknowledgments:

I thank the Creator for bestowing such a wonderful gift in my life--the gift of writing. To my mother, Jean Woodson, my spiritual mother, Bettye Mason Odom, the woman who raised me: Sandra Spears; to my grandmother, Mildred E. Williams who was my first introduction to the Universal Principles; to Sesvalah and Gretta Chamberlain who helped keep my mind growing and expanding to understand what the principles are all about. To my son, J. L.--I love you with all my heart and my one desire is for you to learn that the Universe works in your favor. It is my hope that you will not have to experience the challenges that I have, but when presented with ones of your own, you are spiritually, physically and mentally prepared. To Judy Clarke, Christine Meister, Nancy Wheeler, and Cassondra Heining--you have all been an inspiration. To my last minute angels: Stacey Seay, Sharon Hudson, Linda J. Wilson, Renee Williams, Janice Cochran and Sydney Molare who took time out of their busy schedules to help us get the book finished.

May the Creator continously guide your steps.

Naleighna Kai

FOREWORD
by Christine Meister

For most of my adult life, when asked if I believed in God, my answer was no. But about a year ago, I met a woman named Lissa who asked me that same question and my answer was "not exactly." When Lissa asked me what I meant by that, I had to really think about it. And I realized that, while I don't believe in the traditional, structured-religion version of "God," I do believe in "something." I believe that things happen for a reason. I believe in being in the right place at the right time. I believe that what goes around, comes around. I believe that when we are the most in need of help, it sometimes comes to us from unusual sources. And I believe that we are often presented with opportunities to improve our lives and ourselves, but we have to be willing and able to see those opportunities for what they are — even if they appear in the form of a problem or insurmountable hurdle.

Those beliefs combine into my own unique version of what can only be called Faith. Faith that *there are* forces at work larger than myself.

This book contains true stories about people who have their own Faith. These stories show how that Faith worked in many different ways--everything from putting a roof over a needy person's head to helping another find the path to healing the scars left by a childhood of abuse and neglect. These little glimpses into the lives of real, every day people show us how, even if we think we don't have Faith, it comes and finds us. We just don't always recognize it for what it is.

I have a problem with even the concept of praying for material goods. Instead, I pray for strength. I pray for courage. I pray for wisdom. I pray for the ability to see opportunities when they are presented to me.

Even though the stories in this book sometimes seem to indicate prayer for specific material goods, the real bottom line is these prayers were answered by the ability to *see* opportunities when they arose, or by having set things in motion by some seemingly unrelated action.

Talking about your problems with others can open up opportunities. Asking for help is not a bad thing, we all need help from others, but can't be afraid to ask for it. Sometimes talking about a problem or situation can, in and of itself, lead to possible solutions or answers. The power of the spoken word should never be underestimated.

So whatever you believe in (or don't believe in) – Karma, The Creator, the energy of the universe, the power of Chi, your inner voice, Allah, the collective human spirit, instinct, communing with nature, Jahweh, meditation, finding your center, therapy, whatever – read this book with an open mind and open heart.

The very nature of being human makes us look toward something outside ourselves for the answers that usually lie within. Most of us just need to have the light turned on so we know where to look. And that is exactly what this book does– turns on the light.

--Christine Meister, author of *Make Up Your Own Mind*

"We are all students of the Universe, each one searching for the recipes of life. And within this book you are given samples of how life could be when you . . . *Speak it into Existence.*"

--Ehryck F. Gilmore, author of *Why Am I Stuck:*
The Science of Releasing Yourself From Being Held a Mental Hostage

A message from Sesvalah . . . .

"Life or death is in the power of the tongue."

In other words, we live by what comes out of our mouths. We can have health or sickness, joy or sadness. We also must watch our thoughts because they are seeds for the words that create the life or path we follow.

I remember when I first became aware of this principle and attempted to watch my words; I thought I was doing pretty well. I had declared that I needed a vacation—one that would cost me very little if anything.

My very good friend had planned a trip to Colorado to visit an opera singer who was performing at a yearly music symposium. Along with another close friend, she invited me to come at no cost.

When we arrived in Colorado, the breathtaking view of the snow-capped mountains proudly displayed Mother Nature's artistic hand. The trees dressed in rich shades of green blended wonderfully with the flowers that grew randomly in the meadows and on the hillsides. We could see the sky and its picturesque clouds almost everywhere we looked; there was no pollution to block the magnificent view.

Having some time before we were scheduled to meet our friend, we pulled over to the curb and started making small talk. My health-conscious girlfriend said that one of my favorite foods was garbage.

I jokingly yelled, "Well I don't care! Give me some more garbage." Not thirty seconds later a person missed the waste receptacle just a few feet away and dropped a bag of garbage into the van window right next to me.

I glanced at my friend and she looked back at me. We both burst out laughing. It illustrated the power of the spoken word, even in jest. It was the Universe's way of reminding me that although I thought I was doing well watching what I said, I still had a long way to go.

* * *

What do we want to bring to life? What are our words bringing us?

Our words, as well as our thoughts, have tremendous power. Remember, the words the Creator used in the Bible: "I AM that I AM."

We should always speak of ourselves or our intentions in an affirmative or positive way. As we say we are, so we shall be. The words I AM should never be followed or proceeded by negativity: "I am sick." "I am tired." "I am broke." "I don't like who I am." Substitute positive statements such as: "I AM blessed." "I AM healthy." "I AM full of energy." "I AM prosperous." "I AM reaching my ideal weight and size." "I AM experiencing the best that life has to offer."

Instead of saying "I AM sorry," say, "I apologize." It means the same thing without the negative self-label.

We should also choose our words carefully when speaking of others. Remember that we are all created in God's image. Because that is so, we should greet the God in everyone, never using our words to belittle, degrade, anger or shame anyone.

We should also be mindful of how we judge others, something we do, often without realizing what we are doing. For example, I have made the statement that a certain person's look or style was outlandish.

A prime example is the time I SAID something about people wearing those "plastic shower caps"— the ones used to keep moisture in curly perms or waves — in public. I thought, "You know, he (or she) really looks ridiculous."

One day, not long after I was in the middle of getting my hair done when I was called to the hospital to help handle a rape situation. I left the shop immediately. Without thinking, I stepped outside and dashed through the busy Chicago streets with soaking wet hair held in place by one of those "plastic caps."

I tripped on my own thoughts: I had judged people in those "plastic shower caps" without considering that there could be any number of reasons they were wearing the caps.

All of us are guilty of prejudging others. But we need to remember that the way we judge others is the way we, in turn, will be judged. We need to start seeing beauty in people and situations, and stop looking for the negative: "Look at that short skirt, she should be ashamed to wear something like that," or "Now, you know that suit is too small. Why is he wearing that?" and "That (man/woman) may not be ugly, but he/she is very unpleasant to look at" or the classic: "I'm sick and tired of this job," or "My entire paycheck goes to the bill collectors." The more we say things like this, the more we invite negativity into our lives which will keep these statements true.

Instead, we should focus on some beautiful aspect of that person, thing or situation: "My job is a blessing to me." This is true even if we are faced with a mountain of bills. We just have to redirect some of the blessings from our paycheck to us—*before* we pay the bills. I stress this to people all the time.

The members of the worship center I founded tithe, so I explain that after tithing, people need to pay themselves next, *then* distribute the rest among the bills. We don't work every day for bill collectors, we work to make life easier. Bills are a part of life, but they are not the *main* part. Too often we forget that.

We also should never forget who our source is.

The Creator is The Source — not the employer. The Creator is the one who gives the avenues by which lives are made whole. An employer is just a means. Blessings don't always come in the form of a paycheck.

How many times have funds come out of the blue, from unexpected sources? How many times did it happen when it was most needed? How often did someone offer to do something for no apparent reason? We shouldn't limit the Creator's ability to manifest our desires by always looking for it where *we* think.

Each of us is part of the Creator; the creative force and power run through each of us. No matter what color — black, blue, green, purple or polka dot — we're all God's children and we are all one. We have to remember to see that Divinity in every person. The Bible tells us, "God is a spirit, and they that worship him, must worship him in spirit and in truth." So when it states that we're made in the image of God—the Creator—it's the light within us, the "spirit" or "soul" which animates our earthly bodies, which reflects the image of God, not the outer shell, the covering that adorns us.

Our spirit is like a car's engine and transmission — the internal parts that make the car go. The outer shells, whether a van, truck or car, all different makes and models, serve the same purpose — transportation. The same is true about our physical bodies; they are the *transportation* that carry our souls and spirits. The way we adorn ourselves on the outside IS a matter of choice. Those who are spiritually aware recognize this and embrace the oneness of everyone and everything.

Throughout this book, members of the worship center show how Universal Principles have helped them achieve their dreams, goals, and desires — what some call blessings or an answer to prayer — whether they are becoming an entrepreneur, getting the house and/or car they always wanted, dropping pounds, enjoying better relationships with their mates and children or otherwise.

Peace, love, and prosperity will surround us in our everyday lives once the mind starts to see the Creator in everything—regardless of how life seems. Ehyrck F. Gilmore, CH, author of *Why Am I Stuck? Releasing Yourself from Being Held a Mental Hostage*, says every aspect of life is like a recipe. There's a beautiful color picture of the end results, but directly underneath there are step-by-step instructions on how to achieve those results. As with any recipe, some follow the instructions closely, others may add their own personal touch — extra seasonings, or changing the portions to yield larger results.

Life is very much the same way; ingredients like trusting and having faith in God, affirmations, treasure maps, forgiveness lists, prayers, visualization, meditation in any combination can help to achieve the results we desire.

In this book, you will note that I have added a "recipe" to each case or account, explaining the ingredients or mindset, then exploring the results. You can easily apply your circumstances, dreams, and goals to the stories. Either use a spiral bound notebook or the accompanying journal to this book to write out your own personal recipe to change the way you think and change the way you live. Write things down in your "journal of positive change" *before* you move on to the next chapter. After you finish the book, go back and read your notes.

I have added a little personal information about the people sharing their stories—age, occupation, spiritual background—to reinforce the reality that people from all walks of life can overcome challenges such as lack of money substance, sexual abuse, domestic violence, and much more. They all have one thing in common: They learned to focus on their goals and dreams to speak what they needed into existence.

Let's start with Linda . . .

LINDA

CHALLENGE: **HOUSE NEEDS REMODELING**
AGE: **36**
STATUS: **SINGLE MOTHER**
OCCUPATION: **GRAPHIC DESIGNER**
SPIRITUAL BACKGROUND: **BAPTIST**

Linda lived in a duplex in the middle of the block on Merrion Street. The house was in desperate need of repair. The old carpet with worn, frayed fibers barely held together. Linda didn't like carpeting to begin with and it wreaked havoc on her allergies. But when she tried to pull it up, she found the wooden floor underneath even more frightening. She would just have to live with the "dusty rusty," as she called it, until she could afford to get the floors redone.

The paint job her brother charged "the family rate" to complete, looked as though the money went toward cheap, poor-quality paint and very little labor. After a few more repairs — ones that barely corrected the damage a fire that her aunt started in the kitchen during Thanksgiving six years ago while trying to fix her famous dessert — the house was still in need of major work.

Even the wallpaper Linda used to cover up the paint job in her bedroom wasn't quite as vivid or uplifting anymore. The glittering lily pads floating on pale blue waters were downright depressing. Coupled with her house woes, she — along with three hundred others — had just been terminated from her job with the Mayor's Office of Employment and Training thanks to a political maneuver. As the unemployment checks came in, she searched for a job, even registered with a few temporary agencies, but found nothing.

As Linda lay comfortably on her bed reading a novel late one Sunday afternoon, she looked up and scanned the room. "I'd really like to remodel my house, but I sure don't want it to come from my pocket," she said to no one in particular. She sighed and continued reading, hoping to finish the book before dinnertime.

Two hours later, a loud screeching noise made her heart freeze. Then a crash and the ear-splitting sound of glass breaking made her jerk upward. The house shook like an-out-of-control jack hammer.

Linda scrambled off the bed, but froze at the top of her stairway. A shiny black BMW had sped past her shrubs, through the brick front wall of her home, and was heading into her kitchen. The front end lodged in the wall between the cabinets; the rear extended into the living room. The car had stopped mere inches from her son, Brandon, who lay on the floor watching television just as the car hit the building. If she had fixed dinner on time, her mother, son, nephew, and she would have been sitting around the living room.

The driver, a tall man with dark, wavy hair pulled back into a long ponytail, stood with blood pouring from a gash in his forehead. He shook himself slowly as though trying to erase what happened.

Linda glanced to her right. The evening sun now gave a clear view of her destroyed living room through a bigger picture window than safety would allow. She no longer needed a front door. Her neighbors strolled across the street and from down the street as though a dinner bell had sounded.

The acrid smell of burnt rubber blended with the white powder layering the room. The gurgling sounds of the water she had put on the stove for rice mingled with the sounds of the neighbor's feet cutting across her front lawn.

The warmth of her mother's hand on her neck startled her. Linda followed her mother's gaze to the driver who passed behind a crowd of people, staggering like a man who had a few too many drinks. Then suddenly, he turned, walked back to the car, opened the glove compartment, and peered in. Then he reached behind the black leather driver's seat and pulled out a silver gun and a black pouch. He didn't bother to wipe the blood away or attempt to keep it from dripping into his left eye. He ran out of the opening where her living room window once stood, almost tripping over the bright red bricks laying on the freshly cut lawn.

When Linda was able to move, she went to the car, checked the glove compartment, and found the registration. The car belonged to a woman. The glove compartment also held a picture of the driver holding his . . . girlfriend? Definitely during better times.

The owner was only nineteen years old and drove a brand new BMW? Add that to the fact that the driver took a suspicious-looking bag and the gun and ran away from the scene and Linda knew plenty about the *source* of the income.

The police towed the car from inside the house. Linda called her insurance company and a board-up service came out to cover the broken window and wall, blocking out the cool night air and white full moon.

Two hours later, Linda and her family had cleared away as much of the debris as possible. She served dinner and thanked the Creator that her family was safe.

Because the car had minimal insurance, it didn't cover the damage to the house, so Linda's homeowner's insurance repaired the damage.

Everything Linda wanted remodeled in the house was done—all the floors sanded, kitchen painted and re-tiled, living room windows and walls fixed, new furniture, new shrubs, new vestibule. She even had new windows for the entire house because the old ones weren't up to code. The insurance company had to make all of them uniform, not just replace the damaged ones.

She only vaguely remembered her statement a few months earlier, but the insurance paid to remodel the house and, as she requested, it didn't cost her a dime. Everything had been an exchange on paper.

She realized the outcome could have been far different. Her son could have been hurt or killed; the driver could have shot them so that they couldn't identify him.

Linda learned to be more specific in her requests after that.

On the other hand, had Linda not kept up the premiums on her homeowner's insurance, even while unemployed, the results could have been disastrous.

Affirmation

Divine love always has and always will supply all of my needs." When we make up our own affirmation, we must always add, *"in peace and harmony."*

Speaking it into Existence

Words, words, words . . . they impact our lives in every way, yet most of us are unaware of what we are creating. Linda's words, "I want the house remodeled, but I sure don't want it to come from my pocket," started a series of events that eventually led to the end result she wanted. Her words had power. And so do ours.

How many times have we said, "He's a pain in the neck," or "She makes me sick," and later wondered if we'd slept wrong because we had a crook in the neck, or a strange unexplained pain? Simple things. Negative things. *We must examine our words. Whom are we allowing to bother us? What situation are we allowing to overcome us?*

Before I really paid attention to my words and those of others, I had a friend who always said a particular person made her "butt hurt." Sometime later she started having "butt pains." (I won't go into detail here, but you get the point). Her words were simple enough, but she still felt the result of misplaced words.

It is so very important to realize our future is created in our present — by our words, attitudes, and thoughts.

I teach that we should accept every challenge as a blessing in our lives and not the tragedy it may seem at the time. Even though it may not look like it, feel like it, taste like it, or smell like it, we must continue to speak the blessings into existence — even through the hurt, pain or confusion — knowing that our consciousness will open and broaden so we will begin to see the blessings that God, the Creator, has given us.

Personal recipe

Pull out your personal journal or the Speak it into Existence journal. Take a moment to jot down information that came to mind as you read this chapter. Then write down your own formula for speaking it into existence. It can be an affirmation, Bible verse, mantra, etc., but it should be something that you'll use everyday until you see your desire come into existence.

MARIE

CHALLENGE: **NEW CAR**

AGE: **34**

STATUS: **SINGLE**

OCCUPATION: **TRAVEL CONSULTANT**

SPIRITUAL BACKGROUND: **METHODIST**

Marie sat at the steering wheel of her 1986 Oldsmobile Regency Ninety-Eight, which was held together by spit and the street. Tired of sinking money into the heap, Marie wanted a new car — pronto!

She'd had to use the heater so much during the miserable winter of 1999 that it stopped working properly. She couldn't afford to get it fixed and had to drive with one hand on the wheel, the other continuously clearing frost from the windshield. She tried letting the car warm up for several minutes before driving, but that didn't work either. By the time she arrived at her destination thirty minutes later, the car was just "thinking" about getting warm.

One night as she went to bed, frozen like a Good Humor Popsicle, she muttered, "We REALLY need a car, but I can't really afford a note right now." She went to sleep, praying she would thaw out by morning.

Later that week, Marie talked to her brother Evan. He had a Geo Tracker but didn't like to drive it in winter and had purchased a Sonata. He let Marie use the Tracker. All she had to do was pay the insurance and maintain the car. No car note! It was truly a blessing.

Marie drove the Tracker until she was on her feet and able to buy her own car. Later she was able to help her brother when he needed her. . .

Evan sold the Tracker not long after Marie returned it, leaving him with only the Sonata. He lived with his mother, Sylvia, and let her handle his finances; he turned over his paycheck to her and she paid his bills. If Sylvia needed to borrow money (which was quite often) she could take what she needed without having to ask and she always paid him back. However, as it turned out, she had trouble balancing her own checkbook, so keeping Evan's checkbook straight became a major problem because she constantly borrowed from and returned money to it.

One year, just two months before Christmas, Sylvia skipped three car payments — October, November, and December — thinking she'd make them up the next month.

She didn't tell Evan, nor was she able to make arrangements with the car company. because she wasn't listed on his account. She finally sent in a single payment in January, but by then it was too late.

Evan stepped out of the house to go to work one morning and his car was gone. Vanished. He thought it had been stolen; someone must have figured a way around the hi-tech alarm.

The car turned up in the hands of the repo man. Though upset, Evan didn't make a scene. He just focused on what to do next, mainly — not missing work. Sylvia was also frustrated. She didn't understand why they took the car, especially since she'd sent in a payment.

Marie tried to make her mother understand that while she sent in *one* car payment, the contract stated that the finance company would take back the car if Evan missed even a *single* payment. By the time she sent in the check in January, she was already *four* payments late. When she didn't make arrangements or tell Evan what was going on so he could make arrangements, he defaulted on the loan and the finance company took the car.

Marie called the finance company to try and straighten things out, offering to pay all back payments plus the one for the following month at once, but they wouldn't cooperate.

Before the car debacle, Evan had A-1 credit. Sylvia had done more than just cause him immediate transportation grief — the repossession would come to light and could work against him if he decided to buy a house or make any other large purchase.

Evan never said a cross word to his mother; that was jus his nature. He believed that a car wasn't worth going ballistic. That's why Marie thought that she had to help him. It wasn't Evan's fault. (*Although if he paid his own bills ...*)

Marie remembered how she had walked into a dealership a few days before she returned Evan's Tracker, put her hands on the car she wanted and said, "I'm driving off with this car, low payments, no down payment, regardless of my credit."

Marie was first approved by a company who wanted to charge astronomical rates. She didn't sign. The finance people tried again, and again, until they were able to get payments she could afford. Two hours later, she drove off the lot in her Oldsmobile Aurora smiling and thanking the Creator. The payments were right because cars hadn't been flying off the lot that week and the salesperson had been eager to make the sale.

For two years, Evan had let her drive his Tracker practically for free. The day after his car was taken, Marie took Evan to the place where she bought her car and had him put his hand on a car and say, "I want this car or one that is better."

But in spite of all their fancy talk and promises, the dealer tried to put Evan into an old luxury car or a later model compact car.

Marie's brother was disappointed and so was she. She turned to Evan and said, "Something we did here didn't work. Evan, let's focus on something better. Give me a couple of days."

Marie searched the Internet and found a car at a dealer in the city instead of the suburbs where she purchased her car. She picked Evan up from work and they went to meet the salesman. They laid everything on the line. Unfortunately, the car she had seen advertised online had already been sold.

Evan was becoming frustrated. He had three jobs and getting to each one on time was impossible on public transportation.

Marie walked through the car dealership, put her hand on the car her brother wanted, and said with conviction, "We want this car or better." Then Evan wrote down his own personal affirmation and stuck it in the sun visor of the car.

The car was a newer model than Marie's; it was priced much higher than Evan would be approved for after the repossession of his last vehicle, but he wanted that car. So he filled out the paperwork anyway.

The next day the salesman called Marie and told her, "We're detailing the car so you can come pick it up later."

When she went to the dealer, she was hit with the shock of all times — the car was *theirs*. In order for the loan to go through, she — with not-so-good-credit, and already buying one car on credit — would have to co-sign. Marie sat in the salesperson's chair and roared with laughter as she looked over the paper work again. "Whatever floats the boat."

The finance company wouldn't approve them as brother and sister. So the salesman left the relationship section blank and the finance company put them down as *husband and wife*.

When Marie protested, the told her, "No harm; it's all just paperwork. And the deal is finished. The car belongs to you now. Six months from now, he can refinance it put it in his name only. But at least he's driving it right now and that's the point."

Marie, wanting to surprise her brother, called her sister Angela to drive her car while Marie drove her brother's new car off the lot. Evan's car was better than hers and his payments were lower. *And* he had an alarm system and heated seats, too! The Aurora was the exact color he wanted — dark on the outside — dark on the inside.

Marie pulled up in front of, what Evan called "job number two." and strolled in. The smell of grilled onions and char-grilled Polish sausages made her mouth water, but dinner would have to wait. Evan's back was to Marie so she yelled over the noisy conversation and music. "Hey, you with the funny hat on, I need you to come look at my car. I think something's wrong."

Evan turned around and paused. "You just got that car. How could something be wrong?"

"Trust me. *Something's* wrong."

When he saw the car, he frowned, then his lips widened into an ear-to-ear smile and he hugged her like a kid at Christmas.

"What's wrong is that you don't have the keys yet," Marie told him as she placed them in his hands. He held her hands and the keys, his look relaying every bit of emotion that he felt. The glaze of unshed tears told her everything. Evan seldom cried — she couldn't remember a time when he had. She sighed and told him, "The payments include disability insurance, and warranties."

He already knew it was a better car than what he had before. As her brother sat in his black car smiling and still shocked, Marie told him, "While driving here, a note fell from the sun visor. I picked it up and flipped it open at the first red light. It was the note you wrote and left inside when we first saw the car." Marie gave Evan the note with his choice of affirmation written in his scribble. It said, "The Lord is My Shepherd and I shall not want."

The salesman was able to pull off the loan approval because Marie's recently purchased car wasn't on her credit report yet. The way they wrote the car note, the payments showed on Evan's credit so it would rebuild his credit rating and by the time he was ready for something new, he wouldn't need Marie to co-sign.

One week after Evan lost his car, he was in a new one.

Marie was pleased to see the power of the spoken word work for her again.

*C*hallenge:　Holding onto the old, blocks the way for the new.

*A*ction:　When we want to attract something different or new, we have to let go of the old — clean out our refrigerator, give away our old clothes, change our attitude about ourselves or others. Change — Change — Change. As we are doing this we need to say: I release all worn-out conditions, thoughts, situations, and things in my life. I release, anger, pain, etc. and I accept love, peace — my new car, house, (or whatever you desire).

Evan's car experience was proof that the Creator gives us what we need when we need it, regardless of what *we* think about the obstacles, which are God's opportunity to let us know he hears our prayers. Only God can place people, circumstances, and situations in the right place to bring about our heart's desire, even when things seem challenging.

When God takes care of things, all the details fall into place.

Personal recipe

Pull out your personal journal or the Speak it into Existence journal. Take a moment to jot down information that came to mind as you read this chapter. Then write down your own formula for speaking it into existence. It can be an affirmation, Bible verse, mantra, etc., but it should be something that you'll use everyday until you see your desire come into existence.

TINA

CHALLENGE: LETTING GO OF PAINFUL EPISODES/FORGIVENESS
AGE: **25**
STATUS: **HAPPILY MARRIED**
OCCUPATION: **COMPUTER TECHNICIAN**
SPIRITUAL BACKGROUND: **ISLAM**

The sun's bright rays fell on Tina and fellow members of Prayer, Praise, and Faith as they gathered on Rainbow Beach. The cooing of the seagulls and the rushing sounds of Lake Michigan eased the heaviness in her heart. The sea-foam green waters were the perfect place for a Forgiveness Ceremony.

Teal blue, fuchsia, purple, metallic gold, and silver balloons were tethered to the metal arm of a folding lawn chair.

Members of all ages and ethnic backgrounds dressed in white summer outfits walked across the sand, praying and lifting their voices in praise.

Each one stopped at the long wooden picnic table and wrote out his/her list of people and situations to forgive. Tina's list filled the front and back of the paper.

"Each one choose a balloon. Pick a color you like best," Sesvalah said, her soothing voice carrying just above the sound of the waves lapping at the shore. Her long flowing gown enveloped her small frame.

Tina chose a silver balloon and held the blue string tightly in her hands. Each member had a balloon in one hand and a folded sheet of paper in the other.

"I want you to tie your lists to balloons," Sesvalah told them.

Several moments later the group followed Sesvalah through the gritty beige sand toward the water where the sand was packed tightly by the moisture.

Sesvalah led them in a brief prayer, then said, "Now we can release the balloons, and with them all anger, resentment, pain, lack and limitation, self-loathing, and anything else that you might be holding onto that is holding you back."

Tina's balloon stalled, while everyone else's lifted and flew up into the light blue, almost cloudless sky.

Sadly, Tina's balloon dragged along the sand in the *opposite* direction. Her list was so heavy that her balloon moseyed along like a kid who would rather play in the park than go to school — no matter the consequences.

Tina's heart felt heavy. As Tina's balloon hit the concrete wall that separated the sand from the bike path and the grass Sesvalah came to stand next to her. The balloon began to rise. Tina smiled. The silver balloon once again got stuck, this time in the electrical wires overhead; it was still far from being away and out of sight like all the others.

Tina frowned. "Sesvalah, my list isn't going anywhere."

"But it's off the ground."

"You would think to say that. But it didn't go anywhere."

Sesvalah chuckled. "It's in the power lines. It needed an extra charge."

Tina gave Sesvalah's hand a gentle squeeze. "Only you could find something good out of it."

"And now you can to. Let it go. Release it mentally and everything will be fine. The balloons are only symbolic. What you release from your heart and mind are the true signs of forgiveness."

*R*elease: the very process of letting go — sometimes we must do a symbolic release in order to achieve our goals.

*A*ffirmation: I am willing, ready, and able to release in peace and harmony I am free.

Action:

Visualize a bouquet of balloons with a word, trait, belief or attitude you no longer need written on it. Separate a balloon and print the word judgmental. (Remember as we judge someone else — we judge ourselves.) Then we see ourselves holding the balloon in the process of letting things go. We might say, "I release and let go of any tendency to be judgmental. I forgive myself for past judgments. I am free and so it is."

Use balloons to continue releasing whatever needs to be shed. I don't suggest releasing people — although it may be tempting. Instead release inharmonious relationships or abusive relationships. God, the Creator will bring about the change.

When we begin to let go of that which is holding us back and prepare to grow in our next stage of spiritual growth, we should begin to thank the Creator that we are becoming ambassadors filled with Christ Consciousness. Begin to say, "I thank you Lord that I am able to stand and say to the lack and limitation when they appear. I have Faith and I will not accept any negative thing in my life. I will not believe lack and limitation exist in my life because where God is, there is only abundance. And even though it doesn't look that way, I know that my God has already prepared a table for me in the presence of my enemies."

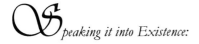Speaking it into Existence:

Lack and limitation are our enemies. Anger and resentment are our enemies. We bring on many of our problems and challenges. None of the outside challenges are stronger than the ones we carry within. We must release those enemies within, begin to let go, and let the presence of God, the Christ Consciousness, take their place.

We've been indoctrinated from childhood to keep those enemies with us. Now we must say, "God I don't want to live with those enemies inside. I release them, I'm letting them go and giving them up to you to baptize, change them around, lift them up, and bring them into the light. Those old ways and parts of me are gone; power-packed divine love has replaced them. That love can do anything but fail in my life.

"Lord, you said that we were made in your image and in your likeness and that my temple was where you reside. So I thank you Lord that this temple is sanctified and purified and that it will walk through anything and survive because that was your promise to me — to all of us."

ersonal recipe

Pull out your personal journal or the Speak it into Existence journal. Take a moment to jot down information that came to mind as you read this chapter. Then write down your own formula for speaking it into existence. It can be an affirmation, Bible verse, mantra, etc., but it should be something that you'll use everyday until you see your desire come into existence.

MILDRED

CHALLENGE: LACK OF MONEY (SUBSTANCE)

AGE: **35**

STATUS: **SINGLE MOTHER**

OCCUPATION: **LEGAL ASSISTANT**

SPIRITUAL BACKGROUND: **CATHOLIC**

One day after paying my bills, I found myself having to stretch $100 until the next pay day fourteen days away. No easy task with a teenage son who put away food as though the last supper was three times a day.

I was drained from working long hours in a boring and tedious job. I finally got fed up and said, "I want to retire from corporate America by the time I'm 35. I want my own company, a business that I love and I want to work on something that I love doing."

I didn't know what I would do to make a living. I was 33 years old and still didn't know what I wanted to be "when I grew up."

I met this guy on the Internet. He wrote poetry to me and I wrote back to him. Then he started sending stories which he would begin, then have me finish. Later the stories and poetry became longer and more sensuous. When I started to tap into my creative side, I couldn't stop writing.

I used the stories we wrote to each other and blended in my life story, then I added another woman's story and a portion of my Internet friend's life and wrote a novel in three months.

My aunt read it and she, along with several close family members asked, "Why should we wait for someone else to publish it? We can do it ourselves."

My brother was already working several jobs, but he took on two more at a nightclub to help start a publishing company.

My mother sold her house and moved into my suburban home and we all began to do research on how to produce and market the book. With the help of a best-selling author, who was also a former classmate, we found an editor, a cover designer, and a printer. Then all it took was finding out what we needed to do to make the book available to the public.

With each of us doing a portion of the office work, licensing, promotions, contracting, finding freelancers, contacting newspapers and magazines, and lawyers, everything fell in line to get the book to the printer. A few weeks later we needed funds to finish paying the printer, but by then everyone was tapped out.

I worked at a law firm and two weeks before the books were to be printed, the lawyer I worked with had to prepare for a major trial. Normally paralegals and associates helped out, but for some reason, on this case they wouldn't put in the necessary overtime. I hadn't worked any overtime all year because I used all my extra time building my business, but I ended up staying for this new project and became the copy center, secretary, paralegal, and everything else he needed to get ready for trial. I worked 92 hours in a five-day period, practically spending the nights there and having my sister bring in some clothes everyday. To say I was bushed would be putting it mildly.

Everything worked in my favor. The time I worked would reflect on the paycheck I would receive four days before we needed to pay the printer. We didn't have to take out a loan.

The first printing sold out within two months and the process brought my family closer.

I continued to write, and had produced two more books by the time the first one came out. I moved those new projects along as if we had the money. I called my karate instructor to ask permission to include his name and the name of his business in a new book. He asked "So how are the book sales coming?"

"We're sold out and it'll take the stores almost 120 days to pay. Now I have orders but no books."

He was silent for a moment and then said, "I know the only thing that could stand between you and success had to be cash flow. How much does it cost to reprint?"

I gave him the figure.

"You can pick up a check on Monday."

His offer made me sit down and put some numbers together to figure out how to get the money back to him. What I discovered was an investor's gold mine! I could afford to pay back the loan plus twenty percent interest and still make a load of money for the company. And with our distribution plan, we could give him his money back in *three* months time!

I sent him a proposal just so the numbers and time frame would be clear. He consented to reprint the first one, then also said he would pay for printing another project and that was a blessing. When I told one of my church members that we would be reprinting through the help of my karate instructor, she wanted to know how it happened. When I told her, she volunteered to help print one of the other books. Investing was a hobby and she knew my determination and had followed the success of the first printing.

Thanks to their help — and great sales — the company is debt-free. Every book that gets printed doesn't take money out of our pockets and the company has become a prime money-earning opportunity for individuals who want to help. My family has been able to travel as part of their roles with the company.

Time, energy, and promotions sell the books and we have gained the experience to make every novel that we decide to print a success.

Mildred is set to retire one month before her next birthday

*C*hallenge: Lack of money substance

*A*ffirmation: Begin to examine your thoughts — pay attention to your words. Are you praying for abundance and at the same time speaking lack into your life? — "I don't have enough money." Remember always — the power of the spoken word directs the flow of your life. Whichever thought has the most power is the thought that brings results.

*ffirmation:*

As we stay on target, as we continue to say to those negative thoughts that come, "The Creator is taking care of me. The Lord is My Shepherd and I shall not want. My cup is running over with abundance, joy or excellent health, and God will walk with me through the valley. God will be with me." Whatever we need, we call forth.

Things will begin to open up for us. Money will begin to come. People will come into our life and bring us substance. They'll bring us what is needed — they'll bring us clothes if we need clothes.

Be steadfast through living by faith and not by sight. Because if we live by sight, we'll begin to fear wars and rumors of wars. We'll begin to fear the *lack* that the media is talking about; we'll become depressed. We'll begin to fear violence. We'll begin to fear walking down the street when we see a man or group of men with bald white heads, or wearing leather and riding motorcycles. "Will they hurt me?" Or it may be a group of young Black men and we'll clutch our belongings that much tighter, wondering, "Oh, my God, what are they thinking?"

On both counts we get caught up in that "race stuff," and forget that we are divinely protected. The Universe will circulate prosperity, protection, good health, or whatever we need — when we focus on the positive end result and not the obstacles or fear that can keep what we desire out of our reach.

*ersonal recipe* —————————————————————

Pull out your personal journal or the Speak it into Existence journal. Take a moment to jot down information that came to mind as you read this chapter. Then write down your own formula for speaking it into existence. It can be an affirmation, Bible verse, mantra, etc., but it should be something that you'll use everyday until you see your desire come into existence.

DENISE

CHALLENGE: **OVERCOMING OBSTACLES OR STUMBLING BLOCKS**

AGE: **29**

STATUS: **SINGLE MOTHER**

OCCUPATION: **TELEPHONE COMPANY CUSTOMER SERVICE REPRESENTATIVE**

SPIRITUAL BACKGROUND: **C.O.G.I.C. (CHURCH OF GOD IN CHRIST)**

Denise's landlord had raised her rent another twenty dollars. She paid more for her two-bedroom apartment than some paid for a three-bedroom home. She would love to own a house, but because her cousin had defaulted on a car loan that she co-signed on, a house seemed out of the question.

After church service one Saturday, Denise trudged into the small second-floor apartment lodged between noisy neighbors upstairs and nosy Amy downstairs. She glanced around, displeased by the colors and style of the place. Denise couldn't decorate the place the way she wanted because her lease said only the landlord could make improvements and he charged more than the professionals. The off-white walls and ugly tan carpet made her feel like she was more of a traveling guest than someone who planned to live there for a while.

"I need a house," Denise said, viewing the place from the middle of her living room. She stormed into her sister's room. "Pack your stuff, we're buying a house."

Her sister, Karen, who also attended the same teaching/healing center as Denise, didn't hesitate. "All right. I'm with that program."

A few days later Denise got a job with Ameritech in their ISBN provisioning center — an hour and fifteen minute commute each way, something Denise wasn't accustomed to, but the money was right. Denise flipped through the yellow pages and picked out a real estate agent and told her everything up front so there would be no surprises. "My credit isn't the greatest. It has one major blight — a car loan I co-signed. There's also a credit card issue." She had allowed someone to rent a car with her American Express card — a car that was never returned.

"Let's pull a report and see what we're working with here."

The next day the real estate agent called Denise at work. "Well, you're right about your credit, but I have a finance man who can work wonders."

Denise knew that her credit required more than just wonders — it needed a miracle.

The agent, Kim, put together a list of some properties in Denise's area so her son could remain in the same school. Later, they walked inside a ranch home on the quiet corner of 141st and Saginaw. The house was warm with an attached, heated, garaged. Unfortunately, once the owners saw Denise, her sister and son, they said "We're just thinking about selling."

The Realtor said, "Well, if you signed a listing agreement, you're supposed to be doing more than just thinking."

That same house was immediately sold to another woman — who just happened to be of the same ethnicity as the owners.

Denise was a little disappointed, but not discouraged. She would have the house that was meant for her.

The agent found another house two blocks away. The two-story black-and-white frame house had four bedrooms, two bathrooms, a living room, dining room, and *two kitchens*. It also had a detached two-car garage with an attic. The property was fenced and there was a huge playground at the end of the block.

The house was perfect. Having just starting a new job meant the earnest money needed to take the house off the market would have to wait a couple of weeks. Several people were looking at the house, which meant it could be sold by the time Denise and her sister had the money.

Two days after Denise decided she wanted the place, she talked about the house, and her mama suddenly asked, "When will you move in?"

"Hopefully we can put together the earnest money to take if off the market in the next two weeks, then we'll have ninety days to find the financing and close the deal."

"How much do you need?"

"$1000."

"I'll get it from my credit union."

Denise was floored. "Mama, you don't have to do that."

"Girl, I'd like to visit you without having to climb all those stairs. I could have a heart attack on those things."

Denise laughed. "I appreciate your help, Mama."

With the Manistee house off the market, Denise and her sister started packing. Days later, Kim, the real estate agent called. "We've run into a bit of a problem. The price of the house is more than what the finance company is willing to go."

"You're kidding."

"I wish I were."

Denise sighed softly. "Will the owners come down on the price?"

The agent sighed. "Nope, and I tried like crazy."

"Let's try for something else."

"All right. I'll call you later."

Denise was disappointed, but knew something would come up. She and her sister looked at other homes and kept packing.

Kim called a week later. "Hey, do you still want the house on Manistee?"

"Of course."

"Well, it's still available."

"At the right price?" Denise asked, perking up.

"Yes."

"How did that happen?"

The real estate agent paused for several moments. "The man who owned it died."

Silence.

"Denise?"

"In the house?"

Kim chuckled. "No, not in the house."

"Whew!"

"He was lonely since his wife died the year before."

Silence.

"Denise?"

Denise swallowed. "In the house?"

"Oh, heavens no! She was ill, and he drank himself to death. He died in the hospital, twenty-three miles from the house."

"Wow."

"So are you still interested?"

"You bet."

"The house costs less than before, plus all the appliances, furniture, and everything in it will only cost you a single dollar. The man's sister who lives in Kentucky wants to be rid of it."

Denise closed on the house exactly ninety days from the date she said, "I want a house."

*C*hallenge: *Overcoming obstacles or stumbling blocks*

*A*ction: "Baptize" the situation as a blessing, although we may not see it at the time. (I always say when confronted with an obstacle or situation, "I am a blessing to [name the situation], and it is a blessing for me. Even though I may not see it or feel it. I ask the Creator to reveal to me the blessing that this situation creates in my life.")

I continue stating this until answers unfold or the "seeming-negative situation" dissipates and actually becomes a blessing.

"My God shall supply all of my needs according to His riches in glory. Thank you God for leading me to my perfect dwelling place, at the perfect price and in the perfect location. And so it is."

*ffirmation:*

Faith without works is dead. We can have plenty of faith, but if we don't get up and do the work we may not achieve our goals. So instead of saying to the Creator or speaking out into the Universe: "Okay, I want to do _____, what are you going to do about it?" We begin to stay in the consciousness and say, "It's time for me to make a change."

It may be that we just need to clean out our desk drawer in order to bring about that new job. Or that we need to buy a set of glassware to celebrate our first night in our desired new home. Sometimes all it takes is cleaning our house while saying, "I'm ridding myself of all this stuff because it's holding me back. I'm ready to make this change in my life."

ction:

It doesn't have to be a big action, but we do have to take *some kind of action.* Decide on a goal, desire or prayer request and begin to thank the Creator each day with a heart filled with gladness. Joyfully anticipate the results. Then think of something (action) that can be done that will bring that desire that much closer.

*ersonal recipe*

Pull out your personal journal or the Speak it into Existence journal. Take a moment to jot down information that came to mind as you read this chapter. Then write down your own formula for speaking it into existence. It can be an affirmation, Bible verse, mantra, etc., but it should be something that you'll use everyday until you see your desire come into existence.

There are many ways to express our desires and to bring them to fruition. Some use prayer, affirmations, or meditation; others use creative visualization, treasure maps, or list-making. Each one is an outward expression of belief, but all achieve the same results: to bring about that which we desire or need.

TEHUTI

CHALLENGE: VACATION "AT LITTLE OR NO COST TO ME."

AGE: 45

STATUS: HAPPILY MARRIED

OCCUPATION: REAL ESTATE EXECUTIVE

SPIRITUAL BACKGROUND: AUSAR-AUSET

One day members of Tehuti's Master Mind Group held a meeting in which he requested the Master Mind (God) to bless him with a vacation to the Islands. Ten minutes after the meeting, a female friend walked into his living room and asked, "Does anyone want to go to Jamaica?" Immediately three in the group, including Tehuti, stood and said "yes"; eight others stayed on the couch looking skeptical.

As she wrote the names on a piece of paper, she said, "The hair care company I work for planned a convention in Ocho Rios and has space for twenty more people at a discounted rate. The trip includes air, ground transport, and hotel accommodations."

Within three months Tehuti and his wife were enjoying a fantastic five-day Jamaican vacation at a total cost of only $500.

Tehuti "spoke the word" of his intentions and it manifested faster than even he could imagine.

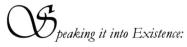peaking it into Existence:

God answers our spoken prayers (requests, pleas) as well as those that are silent. We must release the prayer or request, knowing that "while we are yet speaking, the Creator has already answered."

When we pray we must expect a door to open, a mountain to be removed or an earth angel to be put in place. Therefore, we must look for the signs, listen to the still small voice, and walk through the door as it opens.

Tehuti did not know he would be able to afford a luxury vacation for his family. But he believed it could happen and knew that the power of God, the Creator, could supply the how, when, and where.

It is our responsibility to be aware of the signs and move into action. When the young woman stated she had a trip available, he did not hesitate — he moved into action.

A*ction:*

Cut out pictures of the place we want to visit. Place them in an area where we can see them everyday and thank the Creator for the vacation. We must see ourselves there enjoying the summer breeze, tasting the wonderful cuisine, etc.

A*ffirmation:*

Thank you God for my perfect trip to _____ at little or no cost at all. God is my travel agent and all is well.

P*ersonal recipe*

Pull out your personal journal or the Speak it into Existence journal. Take a moment to jot down information that came to mind as you read this chapter. Then write down your own formula for speaking it into existence. It can be an affirmation, Bible verse, mantra, etc., but it should be something that you'll use everyday until you see your desire come into existence.

JEREMY

CHALLENGE: **ABANDONMENT, FORGIVENESS**

AGE: **14**

OCCUPATION: **HIGH SCHOOL STUDENT**

SPIRITUAL BACKGROUND: **BAPTIST/ISLAM/SCIENCE OF MIND**

Everyone on this earth has a father. It's a fact, whether they know him or get a chance to meet him. I didn't know that I had a "real" one until I was four years old. He just showed up at the house one night and I remember he was riding his bike. He had curly hair, a thick mustache, and looked thinner than the mental picture I had of him. I wondered why in the world my dad was lighter than I, until my mother explained that he was Mexican. That also explained why I had curly hair and was a little lighter than my mom. I was happy to find out who my father was.

It wasn't until a little later that I saw the rest of my Mexican family even though they lived only five blocks away. I was still young and remember it was Christmas time when they just popped out of nowhere and showed up at my house. I later learned that my grandmother's sister, Alicia, from Mexico, forced my grandmother to bring her to see me.

My mom and dad were not on the friendliest of terms, but they were at least civil. Mom never said negative things about him or kept me from seeing him, but I knew something was wrong.

For a short time, when my dad did show up, we had fun. I thought we weren't spending more time together because he had to work but that wasn't the case. He taught me how to play football and a little soccer, but I liked football better. He taught my cousin, Erica, and me how to play dominoes. He would also take me to family gatherings where I would spend more time with my Mexican relatives.

After a while he slowly faded out of the scene. I would call him, but most of the time he didn't answer — and there were times I knew he was home because I rode past on my bike and saw him through the window. I was hurt. I went to mom and asked her what happened to him, but she didn't know either.

One day my mom took me with her to a courthouse downtown. I didn't know why I was going, but my mom told me I would see my dad there. At the time I didn't really understand the words *child support*, all I knew was that my dad had a sorry look on his face and he wouldn't look me in the eye. My mom later explained that he was there because he wasn't supporting me financially.

It was during the time we were in court that I wondered why my dad wasn't living with us. Mom told me they weren't really on speaking terms. Something had happened before I was born.

When we lost contact for a while I thought it was Mom's fault because of their relationship. She kept telling me that she never told my father that he couldn't visit and that he was doing things all on his own.

One day I got in touch with him, and he acted like he never received any of my phone calls. I left voicemails and he had caller ID, so I kind of figured that he wasn't telling the truth, but as long as I was in contact with him again that was all that mattered.

As I got older, he disappointed me more. I ran away from home twice to be with him because I thought my mom wrong for punishing me when I got in trouble — which was most often because I was angry with my dad and didn't understand his attitude. I was angry with my mother, thinking my father stayed away because they didn't get along. Going through my little "puberty stage" didn't help. Hours later after showing up on his doorstep, I ended up right back at my mother's house because he couldn't take care of me. No that's not the right word — he *wouldn't* take care of me.

Everything else — the unreturned phone calls, lack of visits, failure to keep his promises — were things I mostly forgave him for, but there is one day I will never forget — Father's Day. I called my dad three days before and asked him if I could take him out. We agreed on the time and place. I had planned everything. When Father's Day came he never showed up. I was hurt to the point I went to my room and cried.

My mother had been on her way out the door for lunch with my aunt and grandmother. She told them, "Let's wait until his father comes to pick him up." She knew he wouldn't show.

After I stopped crying I went to lunch with them instead of my father. They tried their best to make me laugh, but I was really hurting inside. I was a karate champion, a straight-A (well, sometimes B) student, baseball champion, never got into trouble (most of the time) and didn't drink or do drugs. I couldn't understand why my dad wouldn't love me. I was a good person and his only child.

The day after he stood me up, I called him to ask what happened. He said he was sick. I didn't know what to believe. It could happen, but I'd talked to him the day before and he was perfectly fine.

For four straight years Father's Day was a really big disappointment. The second and third year was the same excuse, "I was sick." I decided to try one more time, but he never showed, so I took a trip over to his house and left his card in the mailbox. I figured that he wasn't home since I didn't see his car.

After I dropped off his card I went over to his next-door neighbor's house and found out something that seriously messed me up deep inside. They neighbor told me that my dad went to California — not for a job, or anything important, he went for a vacation. I wanted to throw a brick through his window, but it wasn't his house, it was his mother's.

At forty-two he had never had his own house or any responsibility — not even for me. I didn't want to see him ever again. I ripped up his phone number and erased it from my head. I didn't think of him again.

When I was in eighth grade, I received a phone call from my Aunt Monica, my father's sister. She was getting married and wanted me to come. More than likely my dad would be there, so I had to think about it. I did something I now regret — I didn't go. Later, I kept asking myself, "Why didn't you go?" It shouldn't have mattered whether he was there or not, I should have been there for my Aunt Monica and Uncle Tony.

My mom took my dad to court again during my freshman year in high school. I didn't attend because I didn't want to see him, but later I asked her if I could read the court transcript that she kept in a folder with my name on it. At first she said no. When I asked again and again, she finally gave in. One thing stuck out — the part when he said that I wasn't his son. It seriously pissed me off. I smiled when my mom asked me if anything was wrong, but I was filled with rage on the inside.

My father wanted to terminate his parental rights and have nothing more to do with me — as if he had really been involved in the first place. I would've had to take a paternity test if my mom's lawyer hadn't undressed the lie my dad told and used "documentary evidence" to reveal the truth.

Finally, when I was fourteen, I got the message and realized I didn't need the headache — or him.

I received an invitation to my cousin Erica's fifteenth birthday party. I missed my aunt's wedding because of him; I wasn't going to miss anything else. I went to their Catholic Church (I forget what kind of ceremony it was, I just remember it was kind of quiet). I was all dressed up and my relatives were telling me how big I'd grown, and how I looked older than my age.

We went back to Aunt Monica's house and I changed into party clothes. I helped set up the decorations and when the party started, I saw a lot of people I hadn't seen in a while. I danced with my cousin's friends. Then I saw my dad. He startled me at first, but after that I pretty much ignored him. When I got tired of dancing I went to the bathroom. A couple of seconds later he entered. I could tell that he was nervous and wanted to talk to me so I said, "Hi."

We didn't say anything after that, so I went out to the bar and grabbed a soda. Then a few minutes later he was right next to me and asked, "How are you doing?" We talked for a bit and I met his dad for the first time. His dad had left his family when my father was a teenager. My grandma Emma had raised five children on her own. I didn't understand why my dad couldn't do better than his own father.

When the party was over I walked outside and he stood right beside me and tried to get back into my life to start another father-son relationship. I thought about all those times he hurt me. I declined, but never said why. I believe he got the message when I never called.

I had to begin to love me and understand how important I am. I also had to understand that my father not bein in my life didn't mean I was not a worthy person. I also had to release the anger and that took talking to my minister, Sesvalah.

Now I realize that even though my dad isn't in my life, I have my mom, my church family, other male role models, like my Big Brother, Chris Mckee, and my karate instructors. I love my dad, but I don't like what he's done, but I can still love him at a distance. And it's okay.

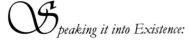*peaking it into Existence:*

Forgiveness is the emotional cleanser, the detox of the emotional body of the soul. We get stuck in lack and limitation and remain in bondage when we are not able to forgive others. Forgiveness removes blocks, disease, and lack of money.

If we need to forgive and release a person, we need to start today. We can write an affirmation of forgiveness on a sheet of paper for the twenty-one days so it becomes a part of our nature. For example, "I completely release and unconditionally forgive and release [fill in the name of choice] to their highest good. And I forgive and release myself to my highest good. Thank you God that it is so."

Or we can visualize the person and say something like (in Jeremy's case) "Dad, I forgive you for not being the father I felt I needed you to be. I release you in Jesus' name to your highest good. And so it is."

God is Divine Love. That means we begin to love who we are because God is inside us. We can't say that we love God if we don't love who we are. So, as we look in the mirror, we have to begin to tell ourselves, "I love myself, because God lives inside of me. I love every part of me, every essence of who I am."

And as we begin to love who we are, it is easy to love our neighbor, which is the second commandment — to love your neighbor as yourself. And as we begin to do that, the whole world begins to open up doors that man cannot close because we are sending out the Love of God. We are becoming the love that God is.

We're being transformed by renewing our mind, by staying in the consciousness that God is, by knowing that as we stay in that consciousness. We can speak to that aparrent or "seeming" situation. "Let there be light. There is no darkness where I am because the light of God lives in me. There is no darkness in this situation because the light of God is in me. There is no darkness in this relationship because the light of God is in me." We can watch the transformation become evident in every area of our lives, watch the way we will be able to stand and touch others, and their light will begin to change because they want to see the light of God in themselves.

Jeremy, a teenager, who like so many others, needed a male figure in his life. He tried constantly with the one he believed should have been that person. As Jeremy began to release and let go, other men came into his life and filled that void. That's what happens when we release the anger and resentment. We are filled with Divine Love, and that love will magnetize and attract that which is for us.

*P**ersonal recipe*

Pull out your personal journal or the Speak it into Existence journal. Take a moment to jot down information that came to mind as you read this chapter. Then write down your own formula for speaking it into existence. It can be an affirmation, Bible verse, mantra, etc., but it should be something that you'll use everyday until you see your desire come into existence.

Leslie

CHALLENGE: **Needs a computer, car, clothes, etc.**

AGE: **15**

OCCUPATION: **High School Student**

SPIRITUAL BACKGROUND: **Science of Mind**

Leslie loved doing treasure maps — a physical form of creative visualization. She would cut out pictures and other representations of things she wanted to bring into her life. She filled her white poster board with pictures befitting a typical teenage girl: Coach purses, watches, clothes, a new bedroom set, and a computer.

She positioned her treasure map in a place where she would see it on a regular basis, but still in a location that was strictly for her use. She continually thanked God for the manifestation of her desires in a perfect way. One by one they begin to manifest from people who had never laid eyes on her treasure map, or even knew that the things they gave her were things she desired. Everything on her treasure map come into existence within a short period of time. Then it was time for a new treasure map!

Treasure Maps

We can purchase a poster board (maybe white for spiritual goals, pink for love and relationships, blue for peace, green for prosperity, or orange for vitality and health) and paste a picture of something that symbolizes the Divine Principle in the center. For example, a Bible or a white dove in the center would signify that everything comes from the Creator.

Write a personal affirmation under the symbol, such as: "The Lord is my Shepherd and I shall not want for any good thing."

Next, add pictures of the things that we want to do, own or be and place it somewhere in the house, bedroom, living room, etc. where we'll see it everyday. Use our affirmation to speak it in existence.

There are many ways to express our desires and to bring them to fruition. Some use prayer, affirmations, or meditation; others use creative visualization, treasure maps, or list-making. Each one is an outward expression of belief, but all achieve the same results: to bring about that which we desire or need.

*P*ersonal recipe

Pull out your personal journal or the Speak it into Existence journal.  *Take a moment to jot down information that came to mind as you read this chapter. Then write down your own formula for speaking it into existence. It can be an affirmation, Bible verse, mantra, etc., but it should be something that you'll use everyday until you see your desire come into existence.*

VEE

CHALLENGE: OVERCOMING DOMESTIC ABUSE/VIOLENCE

AGE: **46**

STATUS: **SINGLE**

OCCUPATION: **AIRLINE CUSTOMER SERVICE REPRESENTATIVE**

SPIRITUAL BACKGROUND: **BAPTIST**

A note about Vee before we hear her story: Vee is another one of my clients who went through counseling before she was finally able to relate her story of being in hiding from an abusive husband for six years. She, too, shared her story with the world in a novel, *Trio* using a character named "Diane."

In counseling sessions, all of my clients — even church members — are encouraged to speak their minds or to tell a story exactly the way it happened.

As a counselor, I expect *all* clients to speak without fear that I, as a minister, will judge them. That being said, I will warn you that Vee's language sometimes borders on being ...colorful. In these instances, some words have been removed, but the context and meaning are intact. I believe it is important for people to know that counselors who are also ministers can be objective and help without infusing religion as the only strategy for success. Now on to her account:

Melvin worked nights so I was able to go out and have fun. I never cheated on him because it was something that I never thought of doing. As far as gambling — my favorite pastime — he really didn't know about it. He believed I always had money saved because I had a habit of saving as much as possible. Little did he know.

Things were all right between us until I decided to go back to school. Melvin wasn't too happy about it, and we had several heated arguments. I finally told him: that this was my life and either I attended business school or we could call it quits. When I got married I hadn't set my own goals, but I did have my own mind. I told him that there were some subjects I wanted to brush up on so I could get a job..

He totally flipped out! He asked me, "What the hell do you need a job for?"

Eventually, he seemed to get over it. I picked up some business courses and completed the hours to get my certificate in business administration. When I landed a job things really became stressed between us.

I worked nights in the records department at a hospital. Melvin still wasn't too happy about the fact that I was working, but I told him I wanted to do it. We argued about it for about three months, until one day, I told him. "Either this is the way it is or it isn't."

"Well, I'm not going to have it."

I looked at the place, which had been spotless before I left for work, and found a bunch of people in my house along with beer cans, bottles, ashes, and cigarette butts. In the kitchen I found dishes everywhere. The food I cooked for our dinner was all gone. *And he wasn't going to have it?*

When I started packing my bags he got all huffy, grabbed my arm, slapped me, and pushed me down in to the chair.

'Oh, no, we're not having any of this sh*t!" We could argue forever, but when he put his hands on me, it was on! I ran to the bedroom and while Melvin tried to figure out why I was going there, his brother tried to head me off. He was too late.

I reached underneath the mattress then ran out of the bedroom. "I'm tired, and I don't need to hear this sh*t every day or have anyone roughhousing me." I held his gun steady in my hand. "Everybody get the f*ck out of my house right now."

My brother-in-law tried to grab my hand, and people stood in a daze trying to figure out what the hell was going on. "My husband and I need to reach an understanding." People weren't moving, and I was done explaining. I pointed the gun toward the ceiling and discharged it — twice.

When the shots rang in the air, let me tell you, people ran out of that house in every direction, about forty going north — like roaches when the lights come on.

Melvin ducked and held his hands high above his head. "Come on, Diane. Now, you know we can talk about this. We don't need this."

"What I need is peace and quiet, and for my husband to support me when I'm trying to do something right. You don't want me to work, but you're laid off and there's no money coming in. How the hell are we supposed to pay the damn bills? I don't need to hear no bullsh*t about not working. I need to hear your plans about trying to find some work, especially since you don't want me to!

"I'm not going to come home every day to find folks all over my house making it dirty and filthy. They ate up everything I cooked and didn't even save me a damn bite! I work, then come home to cook, clean up, and hear you b*tching too. That is not going to happen. Everyone in the house has to get their act together."

I had Melvin's undivided attention for a change. Maybe the fact that I was still holding the gun had something to do with it.

Melvin crawled to the phone and called my mom. "Your daughter pulled a gun on me. She's lost her mind!" The stunned look on his face told me she must have asked him, "What did you do to cause her to lose her mind?"

I couldn't help it — I busted out laughing. *Did he really think my mom wouldn't know me well enough to figure things out?*

She asked him to put me on the phone. "Now, Diane, what are you doing over there? You know that you can't be shooting guns off like that. Unless you're aiming to kill someone..."

That's a Texas rule — guns are for killing, not for threatening. *How could I forget that?* Actually, I didn't forget. I wasn't trying to kill my husband, I just wanted some respect. That's all. Sometimes a tiny woman like me gets more respect with a Smith & Wesson than she can ever get on her own.

After I explained what happened she said, "If you need a break just come over here. And bring the metal with you."

I spent a few days with Mom (along with my trusty .45 caliber friend). When I returned home I was in better spirits, and Mr. Smitty found his way into the nearest river. By then Melvin had a job that he liked, and paid him a little more than his last job.

VEE (SESSION II)
CHALLENGE: JEALOUS HUSBAND/DOMESTIC ABUSE

Soon after that I had appendicitis. During the course of surgery, my heart stopped. My family, and even Melvin, cried as the doctors let them know that they were doing everything within their power to make sure that I came through okay. The doctors later told me that I had to be most stubborn person they ever treated. I didn't give up. I fought to stay on this earth.

I thank the Creator for the tender hand of mercy and for pulling me through. I made a promise to myself that I was going to live life to the fullest. An experience like that makes you think twice about things. It makes you think about what's important. If we don't take care of self, and if we don't love self, no one else can do it for you. And no one appreciates you more than you appreciate yourself.

My recovery time wasn't long because I'm a fast healer, but I never knew being at home could be so nerve-racking. I soon got bored and I was also getting fed up with Melvin. We were arguing about petty stuff.

When I started making trips away from the house, I found out that Melvin was a very jealous person. If I wasn't at home when he called during the day, he would call everywhere he thought I could be, asking if the neighbors or my friends knew where I was and what I was doing.

I finally had to tell him, "I'm not a child. I'm a grown woman and also your wife, but I'm sick and tired of you calling all over the planet looking for me. You're going to have to get out of that. If you can't control your jealousy, then you and I don't need to be together."

He calmed down and things were fine until he came home one from work one afternoon. Jealousy didn't factor into it this time — stupidity took over. I felt horrible when I woke up that morning, so I didn't cook.

Melvin roared at the top of his lungs. "Woman, how come you don't have anything on the stove? I'm hungry."

"I'm not feeling well. If you're hungry today, you're going to have to cook it yourself."

He stormed over to the couch and said, "Look, I want something to eat."

"Then find something in the refrigerator and cook it. I'm not cooking anything today."

He looked in the refrigerator and didn't see anything he wanted, so he went to the store. An hour later, he came back and dumped the groceries loudly on the table and went into the bedroom. I was minding my own business, watching the boob tube, when he came trampling back out. "Woman, I told you I was hungry. I didn't buy those groceries just to be sitting over there on the table looking at you."

I repeated what I'd already said.

In three quick strides he was at the couch, he lifted me by the arm, pushed me into the kitchen, and told me, "Cook something!"

"I'm not cooking anything today."

I went to sit down. He slapped me. Front and backhand. Tears blurred my vision.

"If you raise your hand to hit me again, I'm not going to be responsible for what I do."

Melvin backed off and fixed his own dinner. Around seven he was finished eating so he lay across the bed and went to sleep. I waited until about 9:30 or 9:45 when his snoring said he was in a deep sleep. I opened the door to the bedroom, went in, took that nice, well-greased, cast-iron skillet that he used to fix dinner and commenced to hitting him upside his head.

He woke up startled. "Are you losing your mind, woman?"

I told him no and kept right on hitting him.

He jumped out of bed; I was right behind him — still swinging. With great effort I managed to scream, "You son of a b*tch, don't you ever hit me again."

He ran for the front door.

I was right behind him — still swinging. Melvin had lost his mind earlier. I was doing my best to help him find it and keep it. He fumbled, but finally got the door open and ran out. I was right with him — still swinging. He ran from the house in his bare feet, butt-naked, dick swaying in the wind. And I was right behind him — still swinging.

As he managed to pick up speed, my trusty cast-iron friend and I couldn't stay with him. He banged on the neighbor's door. I'm sure he was a sight for sore eyes. If I hadn't been so pissed, I would have found the whole thing hilarious.

Melvin called my dad, and told his version of what happened.

My dad told him, "You're lying because you wouldn't be outside wearing nothing but sweat and bare ass if you hadn't done something to Vee." Then my dad came over, and I told him the whole story.

Later Dad called the neighbor's where Melvin had made his 'special' appearance and asked him to come over. My dad talked with both of us and told Melvin, "You're going to have to learn to keep your hands to yourself. Don't call me anymore for this foolishness because next time I'll take care of things."

Dad had a nice little collection of what my my mother liked to call "metal;" he had shown the collection of guns to Melvin one day when we were visiting. When he said "take care of things," he meant one of his children would be minus a bullet -- and someone would gain in the process.

My husband called his friends to come pick him up so I could have time to cool off. He called me a few days later and asked if he could come home. After making him wait a few more days, I said yes. All marriages have their ups and downs, and I didn't think these fights were anything special. From that point on, Melvin was the one who did the cooking. He also started sleeping in something to cover his ass. And that was the end of that.

Or so I thought.

VEE (SESSION III)
CHALLENGE: DIVINE PROTECTION/FLEEING AN ABUSIVE SITUATION

We moved to New York, and Melvin's personality totally changed. He became so wrapped up with others; he allowed himself to be used by people with poor intentions and didn't even realize our marriage had practically ended.

After a couple of years in New York, I asked Melvin for a divorce, and he hit me so hard, I was practically immobile for about four months. At that time I was taking classes at another business college, going to work 9-to-5, and maintaining my own business. I had to let everything go while I recovered, which was what he wanted all along. Melvin said he would kill me before he let me have a divorce, and I believed him.

One of his brothers had made the same threat.

His wife made the mistake of returning home after she was away for a few days to repeat her request.

He went into the bedroom, came out with a pistol, and shot her while she sat on the sofa and then used a shotgun on himself wwhile their kids were asleep in their beds.

Melvin let me know in no uncertain terms that there would be no divorce. When I got back on my feet, I began to save every extra dollar I made. I started making plans to leave, but couldn't decide where I would go. If I went home, he would find me, or in anger hurt my family trying to get to me. I had to go somewhere that he didn't know very much about.

I was tired of New York — apartment living, the bitter cold, and the unfriendly environment. It was so different from the openness of Houston and its people. I wanted a house, and I didn't want to hustle to make a living. I wanted my freedom from this man who didn't care anything about me.

Melvin was comfortable with the way things were, and it didn't matter how I felt. I was convenient to him because he was illiterate and I handled all of his personal business and affairs. I wasn't supposed to have any feelings. But I did. I started drinking to ease into sleep every night.

Some months later, I was introduced to Lori through one of the lecturers who was a part of my business. The lecturer asked me to send Lori some tapes so she could transcribe them.

It was so easy to talk with Lori, and soon we were discussing the world. We talked on the phone for about a year before I went to visit her in Chicago.

Melvin protested and we fought about it. He demanded to have all of

Lori's personal contact information before I got on the plane.

I had a wonderful time in Chicago. Lori was very intuitive and eventually she asked what was going on with me and wanted to know why I seemed so sad the first day I got here and looked ten years younger on my second day.

When I explained, she told me that her house was open to me; all I had to do was tell her how to help me.

About thirteen months later, I packed as much as I could reasonably take with me to Chicago.

Lori and I were on the phone at 3:30 a.m. "I wish you could leave right now. Suppose he doesn't go to the Million Man March?"

She had reason to be worried. Melvin had already changed his plans a dozen times, which meant I had canceled and repurchased tickets just as many times. It was a costly process. I think Melvin knew something was up and was reluctant to go, but he didn't want to miss the event either.

While Lori and I were talking, I got the signal that there was another call. It was my husband. He was still in New York. I couldn't believe it! He hadn't left town because the police were keeping the buses from reaching his group in front of the Apollo Theatre. He told me if the buses didn't come within the next thirty minutes, he was coming home.

Shock and fear ran through me. I could barely stand. I hung up the phone and it rang again. I forgot Lori was on the other line. "Lori, he's still in town!" I told her I had to leave right then because there was a good possibility that he would be coming home. There was no way I could unpack all my things by the time Melvin got home, and I really didn't want to. There was no turning back now!

Someone was supposed to help me, but they weren't coming until the time I was originally supposed to leave. I called a cab company and asked for someone to come right away. When the cab arrived I threw some of my bags out of the window because they were too heavy to carry down four flights of stairs. Thankfully, the cab driver got me to the airport in record time.

I hid in the bathroom until thirty minutes before boarding time. I had never been so frightened in my life. If Melvin came home and found me gone, there was more than enough time for him to make it to the airport.

When I tried to board the plane, there was an even bigger problem. I called Lori and let her know the people at the boarding gate wouldn't let me on the plane. Security had been beefed up due to a bomb threat. My ticket was in another woman's name so that my husband couldn't track me.

I didn't have the money to buy a new ticket. I had sent most of my funds to Chicago to secure a new apartment; the rest had been used to pay all those cancellation fees. I would have to wait for the next flight out — twelve hours later!

I didn't know what to do or where to turn. People in general aren't too willing to get involved in domestic problems and I didn't know anyone in New York who could help me.

Thankfully, Lori agreed to purchase another ticket on my behalf. It seemed like an eternity waiting for Lori to get to the airport in Chicago. I called home and sure thing, my husband picked up the phone. Oh, shit! My heart dropped when the flight crew told me they couldn't hold the plane any longer.

At the same time I was being left in New York, Lori stood in line at Midway Airport in Chicago, asking the people in line to please let her go ahead, explaining that there was a domestic emergency and that she had to get a friend on a flight. The people in Chicago were kind enough to let her go and the staff opened up the line early so Lori could buy the ticket.

The customer service people in Chicago called the boarding desk in New York. My flight was supposed to leave at 6:32 A.M. Lori paid for the ticket at 6:31. At the last minute, a sister from the New York boarding desk called to the crew on the plane and had them to open the doors.

She, too, had been in similar circumstances at one point in her life. She understood and she risked her job to help me. I hugged her and was escorted onto the plane. Talk about divine intervention! When I arrived at the airport in Chicago, for the first time in my life I fainted.

When I finally came to, Lori, her son Brandon, and I all hugged before we retrieved my luggage. I don't know how Lori did it, but she got to the airport in half the normal time. I learned later that Brandon forced himself to sleep when the needle hit 120 miles per hour because he couldn't take seeing all those cars going past him that fast.

I didn't notice until we reached the car that not only were Lori and Brandon in pajamas, but Lori was barefoot.

I haven't seen my husband since I left New York. And if fate will be kind, I'll never have to see him again."

After I began counseling I started to heal. Then I made a list of what I wanted to experience in the next relationship. Peace, love, harmony, sexual fulfillment, etc."

*W*riting it into Existence:

After being in counseling for less than a year, Vee released her fears and moved back to Houston where she lives with her mother. She has since learned that her husband, who still resides in New York, has cancer but continues to search for her.

Writing her story was a form of therapy for Vee. Writing has proved a useful tool with many of my clients.

The Creator puts us in positions to begin to heal because we want to be vehicles of love, so we have to release the unwillingness to forgive. We have to release the resentment. We have to release the fear. We have to release the tendency to be judgmental so the healing can begin.

The Creator puts us in places to become the goddesses and gods that we are inside. The God part of ourselves begins to grow.

We have to thank the Creator for the opportunities and the challenges that come so we can become that which we pray to be. Then we can go forth and become walking testimonies. We become walking miracles for other people so they can see what could happen in their lives.

In Vee's case, it was meeting a friend over the phone and moving to Chicago.

 **OVERCOMING FEAR**

Fear takes on many disguises: procrastination, lack of self-love, and other beliefs that make us feel unworthy. An old Native American saying: "A warrior dies one time, a coward dies a thousand times," means that we play a situation over and over in our minds anticipating the worst — rejection, abandonment, abuse, or whatever negative "mind talk" we have conditioned ourselves to believe.

We must remember that it is written that *"God has not given us a spirit of fear, but of power, love. and sound mind."* Sometimes just repeating a favorite affirmation, Bible verse or mantra will assist us in finding the strength to make a change.

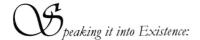 *peaking it into Existence:*

Focus your mind and think about those things that we want to experience in our lives. Begin by saying, "I love and approve of myself and I am ready to change." We need to say these affirmations over and over until they become a part of our consciousness. Sometimes there will be resistance such as forgetting to say the statement when obstacles or challenging situations arise, or maybe just by giving up because we don't see instant results.

We will begin to notice the changes in our lives, some will be quick and others may take more time according to our beliefs and the energy we give toward making the change. Changes may take place in the people who are in our lives, others, who have been a part of our lives for years, may suddenly go away, and new people may come in who reflect and embody the positive change we're making in our lives.

Personal recipe --

In most cases survivors of domestic violence and/or sexual assault are laden with so much guilt, that one of the things theywant to start off with is loving and appreciating who they are as a gift from God. Starting with a simple affirmation such as: I love and approve of myself unconditionally, saying it as many times as possible throughout the day, can work wonders.

ANGELIA

CHALLENGE: **LOST JEWELRY**
AGE: **36**
STATUS: **HAPPILY MARRIED**
OCCUPATION: **SOCIAL WORKER**
SPIRITUAL BACKGROUND: **PENTECOSTAL**

My family gave me a birthday party at my favorite club. A few days before, I had been given an amethyst and silver dolphin bracelet, which I promptly lost while dancing. I didn't realize that it was gone until I got home. Then I kept declaring "there's nothing lost in spirit."

Two weeks later, a friend came to my house. She had been at my birthday party. During the course of conversation she said, "I looked down on the floor while I was dancing and I found the most beautiful jewelry."

"Wow, and I lost some jewelry at the same place."

My friend frowned. "Describe it."

When I described the jewelry, my friend rolled up her sleeve displaying a bracelet — the bracelet that I had lost. "This must be yours."

My bracelet had been returned to me in the most unusual fashion.

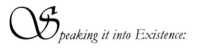*peaking it into Existence:*

Once again, we learn that nothing is ever lost in spirit. I have had several church members who havseemingly lost items that miraculously reappear.

However some readers may think that, as a church member, "Angelia had no business being in a club."

The Essence of God should be in everything that we do and say. Whatever it is, we're doing it with God. Even when we're out there "shaking a tail feather," we're doing it with the thought in mind that God is everywhere, ever-present and in everything. When we take a sip of wine, we're doing it in the mind that God is. God didn't say we couldn't drink, he didn't say we couldn't party, either. But we do those things in moderation.

Remember that Jesus was at the feast. And what was that feast? They feasted for days and weeks. When they partied, they partied for hours and on into days. We have to understand that we must do things in moderation, and do them with God and in the consciousness of who God is.

David of the Bible was a prime example. He lived a "colorful" life and still was the apple of God's eye. He trusted in God implicitly and always gave thanks to the Creator in every situation. We could learn a lot from David:

Praise him with the sound of the trumpet; praise him with the psaltery and harp.

Praise him with the timbrel and dance: praise him with stringed instruments and organs.

Praise him upon the loud sounding cymbals; praise him upon the high sounding symbols.

Let everything that hath breath praise the Lord.

David, a master musician, poet, and leader, danced when the spirit moved him, in other words — partied with the best of them — and was continuously blessed by the Creator.

Personal recipe

Pull out your personal journal or the Speak it into Existence journal. Take a moment to jot down information that came to mind as you read this chapter. Then write down your own formula for speaking it into existence. It can be an affirmation, Bible verse, mantra, etc., but it should be something that you'll use everyday until you see your desire come into existence.

TERRY

CHALLENGE: **DIVINE PROTECTION**
AGE: **22**
STATUS: **SINGLE MOTHER**
OCCUPATION: **FASHION DESIGNER**
SPIRITUAL BACKGROUND: **SOUTHERN BAPTIST**

Once, when my four-year-old son and I went to take the garbage out in my apartment complex, a man pushed in past me as we opened the back door. I told him, "Hey, you can't come through here. You have to use the front door."

He growled, "I came to see my b*tch" and almost knocked me down to get through.

It was the dead of winter and a car stood with the engine running outside and another man at the wheel, waiting. As I tossed my bags into the garbage receptacle by throwing them from the doorway, a small voice inside said, "Don't go back that way. Go around to the front."

I didn't have on any shoes, but I picked up my son and, in my bare feet, briskly walked down the alley to the end of the block.

I didn't have my keys and would have to buzz someone to let me in. I had just moved into the place and unfortunately didn't know anyone. As mistrustful as people in the neighborhood were, it would probably take a while, and I'd probably have frostbite before it was all over. Before I hit the corner of the alley, I heard several gunshots. My pace quickened, then I heard the car door slam.

I plastered my body and my son's onto the bricks of the building so the people in the car couldn't see me when they drove past. My son didn't question what was going on, and didn't squirm. I felt his little heart slamming against his chest. He could tell I was scared.

The car sped past, then slowed down at the corner. The man got out of the car and looked up and down the block as though searching for someone. I realized he was looking for me! At one point he looked right at me. Seconds later, when he drove slowly toward the next block, I ran to the front of my building and frantically pushed the bell for somebody — anybody — to let us in. The lady who lived next to me answered the buzzer.

The next day, I found out that the man who had passed me had killed a woman in the building. If I had not followed my inner voice, he might have killed me and my son on his way back down the stairs.

Speaking it into Existence:

We are Divinely protected . . .

As we begin to follow that still, small voice and allow the Creator to make every decision for us, things begin to fall in place. At the start of each day, we should say, Lord, What should I wear today? Should I wear this? Or should I wear that? Should I go this way or that way? And we'll begin to hear the voice that will tell us what to do and how to do it. We never know if we're preparing for a meeting we didn't know anything about. The voice will wake us up in the middle of the night and say, "Write now." And we won't even know why we wrote that particular statement, but at three o'clock the next day someone calls and asks for the very thing we wrote because God will prepare us if you begin to listen.

As we make a commitment to listen to and spend time with God, we begin to feel the presence of the Creator everywhere we go. There's nothing so important that we can't sit down and give some time to God. We have to keep our commitment to the Creator, God, Infinite Spirit, Christ Consciousness, Holy Spirit, Yahweh or whatever name one may call the Omnipotent force that moves in and through each one of us. Realize that they're all one and the same.

As we make those commitments, we begin to feel the presence of the Creator everywhere we go. Even people, who don't know the Creator is in them, rise up and come to our aid because they recognize the spirit of light within us. As we begin to affirm our beliefs, the Creator walks before us all the time. People can't help but be compelled to do good things for us.

And we can't help but be protected because that, too, is the Creator's promise to us. If we're making a commitment to let the Spirit of God in us become bigger, then we will always protected.

The Christ Consciousness makes us more aware. And as we begin to move, our inner spirit gets there before we do and lets us know that something is getting ready to happen. When we walk in, we'll know what it is--and that's what it's all about--being spiritually aware.

ersonal recipe

Pull out your personal journal or the Speak it into Existence journal. Take a moment to jot down information that came to mind as you read this chapter. Then write down your own formula for speaking it into existence. It can be an affirmation, Bible verse, mantra, etc., but it should be something that you'll use everyday until you see your desire come into existence.

As we know that energy follows thought, so will the actions that are stirred be manifested by your words.

CLARA (story retold by a family member)

CHALLENGE: **Desires a soul mate/husband**

AGE: **49**

STATUS: **Single Mother**

OCCUPATION: **Minister**

SPIRITUAL BACKGROUND: **Apostolic**

Years ago, a minister friend of mine who was a widow with five children, decided that she wanted a husband who would love her and her children. She declared that he would be spiritual, with acceptance of her spiritual path, even if it was different from his. She spoke the words out into the universe, then wrote them down.

She used three principles: the power of the spoken word, vision, and putting the works in place. She began to set an extra place every time she and her children had a meal. The first few times the children didn't pay any attention. Weeks later, they began to question her, "Who's coming to dinner?"

She always answered, "This place is for the new husband that God is sending me." That continued for some time and the children would look at her with strange expressions.

Then one night, a kind gentlemen she had met earlier that week, joined them for dinner. He came back the next night and the next. The children liked him. He later became Clara's loving, supportive husband. He was also a minister, but of a different spiritual background. They supported each other's spiritual journeys by remembering and respecting the fact that there is only one God and one Source. They were together for ten years before he made his transition.

A few years later, she used the same principles and the Creator sent her another helpmate, also a minister, but this time he was of the same spiritual path. He became her assistant minister and they are still together today.

riting it into Existence:

The Bible tells us that his people perish for lack of vision. We must begin to see past what our physical eyes see. The physical eye is limited. Vision gives us the ability to pierce through time and space. We must see what it is that has been placed in our hearts, our dreams, and our minds, regardless of what the limited five senses are saying.

ction:

"Write the vision" [Habakkuk 2:2] Be as specific as possible. To find a mate that loves our children, we must state that. If we want to enjoy traveling, cooking together, etc., write that out, too. When we are finished, we must always thank the Creator for the fulfillment of that desire, but add "in peace and harmony" or some affirmative statement that will ensure that what we desire will come in the best possible manner without hurting or harming anyone else or us. Also state that the perfect mate (or husband/wife) is seeking the ring now. Then do something that is affirmative to the attainment of your goal.

ffirmation:

Thank you God for blessing me with the perfect, Divine mate right now in Divine right action. And so it is."

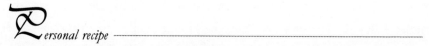 *ersonal recipe*

Pull out your personal journal or the Speak it into Existence journal. Take a moment to jot down information that came to mind as you read this chapter. Then write down your own formula for speaking it into existence. It can be an affirmation, Bible verse, mantra, etc., but it should be something that you'll use everyday until you see your desire come into existence.

MERRY BETH

CHALLENGE: **NATURAL DISASTER**

AGE: **32**

STATUS: **SINGLE MOTHER**

OCCUPATION: **ISDN PROVISIONING CENTER REPRESENTATIVE**

SPIRITUAL BACKGROUND: **SOUTHERN BAPTIST**

Merry and her son, Chris, moved into their new house in Burnham, Illinois, but barely had any furniture after a messy divorce and an electrical fire that ransacked her previous home and took everything.

Two weeks after she settled into the new place, she woke early to go to her job and get Chris off to school. It had been raining all night giving her lawn and the path to her home an extra good soaking.

The rain still hadn't let up by the time she left the house to hit the expressway for work. Rain had flooded most of the streets she tried to travel. After numerous detours, which already made her an hour late, she was still only two miles from home. Traveling the other sixty miles would be a challenge too.

Merry arrived at work three hours later only to find that because of power outages, most of her co-workers hadn't made it in at all. Merry and the few people who were loyal — or brave — enough to show up, were told to go home. She picked up her son on the way in. Schools hadn't fared any better. When she turned to enter Paxton Street, the sight of people wading in what looked to be a river made her heart sink.

She couldn't drive down the street to her house because of the water quickly spilling into the streets. Merry parked a few blocks away, grabbed her purse, and rolled up her blue jeans until they fit snugly around her thighs. After a few brisk steps, Merry caught up with a neighbor and asked, "Anybody for a swim?"

The neighbor didn't bother to laugh or to answer.

Merry couldn't blame him. Joking was her way of dealing with a bad situation, but not everyone could appreciate humor during such hard times.

A block away from her house, Merry pulled off her shoes and held them in her hands. They were already soaked, taking them off was a senseless gesture. What would she find when she got home?

Children played joyfully in the murky water as her son looked on. The newly created Olympic-size pool in the center of the block gave them reason to laugh.

Merry certainly didn't feel like smiling when she thought of the one piece of paper she didn't sign when she purchased her home — the one giving her several thousand dollars in flood insurance coverage. The real estate agent said it wasn't necessary because "it never floods in Burnham." Well either her real estate agent had lied, or someone forgot to tell God to turn off the faucet.

As Merry waded up to her front door, the cold water hit the bottom of her pants cuff. She shivered uncontrollably. Her flowers had floated away, side-by-side with the daily newspaper. Not an especially warming sight.

Merry opened the door to see what little furniture she had left, her, books, clothes, and appliances doing a morbid last dance — the kind one would see to usher out the old and bring in the new. Merry couldn't afford to bring in the new. She'd spent her money to buy hew new home — the one she'd only been in for a month.

Merry trudged to the upper — and drier — level of her home. Heart heavy with worry, she fell into a restless sleep. She woke the next morning to tiny little frogs, no bigger than the tip of her thumb, jumping around as though they owned the joint.

She plopped down on the stairs. Where would she get the money to replace her furniture and clothes? The water department cleaned out the sewers, and only then did the water go away. The mud and the smell lingered like a garbage strike had lasted for months. And there was no way she could live with these little brown frogs. As she looked around, she realized when the water went down inside, it took everything she owned with it.

She slumped on the floor, tears welled in her eyes. "I've always believed in the Creator. I haven't done much praying these days, but I know the Creator is always on my side. Everything will be all right."

Merry scooped up her son and they checked into a hotel.

When Merry could get back into her water-damaged house she and Chris began to peel the damaged paneling off the wall. A knock on the door surprised her. When she looked around, there stood a tall man with blond hair and dimples on the other side of the door. He looked like a good wind could lay him flat.

"Hi, I'm Torrence from FEMA (Federal Emergency Management Agency). I'm here to take a look around and note the damages. We're here to offer assistance."

Merry showed him the house, the furniture, and the damaged furnace. When they'd been through the whole house and the man had taken several notes, he told her, "Okay," we'll be in touch."

Merry didn't think anything more of it — until a week later when she received a FEMA check in the mail for more than $10,000.

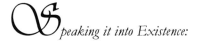

Speaking it into Existence:

It is possible to speak prosperity in our lives just by saying with authority: "Prosperity is here." Money begins to jingle in our purses because we've already laid a foundation with belief and words. Some might even say, "I don't know where it's coming from but my God said my needs would be supplied, so some one or some situation will give me what I need. I don't know how it's going to come, but my God will take care of me."

When I was growing up we were rather poor, and at times things would be so tough that my mother barely had any food. We didn't have a phone, but my godfather just knew when we needed him — the Lord would touch his heart and he would bring us five or six bags of food. No words were exchanged; God would just have him do it. The thing God does for all of His children.

As we begin to keep our minds focused on the fact that we are already taken care of, it doesn't mean we're not going to be tempted and feel a little down. But it does mean that we know that the Lord will lift us back up. And as the Creator lifts us up, when the next down period comes we can say: "I've been there. I don't have to go back that way. There is no depression in God. There is no failure in God. Where God is, there is love. And where love is, there's no room for anything else."

So we must look to the target and look forward to achieving our goals. Ultimately the goal is to achieve Christ Consciousness — where we know who we are and whose we are and we are all Divinely protected — "God's got us covered."

 *ersonal recipe*

Pull out your personal journal or the Speak it into Existence journal. Take a moment to jot down information that came to mind as you read this chapter. Then write down your own formula for speaking it into existence. It can be an affirmation, Bible verse, mantra, etc., but it should be something that you'll use everyday until you see your desire come into existence.

HELENE

CHALLENGE: UNDERACHIEVING SON
AGE: 38
STATUS: SINGLE MOTHER
OCCUPATION: COMPTROLLER
SPIRITUAL BACKGROUND: LUTHERAN

My son was pulling Fs in school, a drastic change from the mostly A and B student that I knew from kindergarten to eighth grade. His attitude toward school had changed; he didn't want to go and was on the verge of dropping out. I was pulling my hair out. He was pulling his hair out. I couldn't understand what was going on.

We had moved from the heart of Chicago to the suburbs to give him a better education. For all practical purposes we thought he was a "done deal" for college. His first year in high school was more than a disappointment. I went from saying, "I'm proud of you," to, "Just please, please, please don't bring me anything less than a "C." Finally it got to the point I resorted to, "If you can get at least a "D" in everything, just pass your classes, I'd be eternally grateful."

I believed that I had failed my child. At one point I thought he might be doing drugs or something. All his teachers told me how bright he was; his test scores were nearly perfect — an A in almost everything, but missing or less-than-perfect class and homework assignments were killing his grades. I didn't know what to do. I even thought of shipping him off to military school or Job Corps. He seemed to become more and more depressed.

Finally, the school counselor had him tested. The scores were so high he had another teacher re-test him with a harder test. The scores were astounding.

But no one — not the school counselor or the school psychologist — could come up with any explanation for his poor grades and lack of interest.

Once, when talking to his history teacher, I found out that almost forty-three percent of the class was failing. When I questioned the teacher he said, "I just give the assignments. They have to answer the questions and turn the work in or they fail. I get paid whether they learn or not."

His attitude toward teaching really ticked me off. The more I questioned him, the more I learned that he didn't teach anything, he just "gave assignments." When I visited the other teachers, I found that most of them had one thing in common: they were just out of college, had no prior teaching experience, and had never interacted with students of different ethnic backgrounds.

When I checked over my son's grades I found that the classes he where he made an effort were taught by older, patient, and more involved instructors. However, his lack of effort in some classes was spreading to all classes. I was stunned when, during one grading period, he received an A in what was usually his worst class and failed the class in which he normally excelled. Something was definitely wrong.

I took my son out of the school and put him in a private school. His grades improved dramatically along with his self-esteem — temporarily. The school had a fundraiser and the students sold donuts to raise money. My son was outside of a mall selling Krispy Kreme doughnuts with three other male students — without my permission. Although there was a teacher along to supervise, she was on the other side of the mall with the female students. So she didn't see the police approach the boys, confiscate the doughnuts, give them citations, and put them into a squad car.

Although the school promised to send someone to court to explain what happened, I was incensed.

It wasn't just that incident that kept me up at night. There was a whole series of administrative blunders and unprofessional behavior, including a judgment call that resulted in the school van being driven by a student.

There was an accident. My son didn't want to tell me, but he had to explain why he was two hours late getting home. That was the last straw. I couldn't spend the next two years wondering whether I would get a call telling me that something drastic had happened to my son at school yet again.

I talked with Sesvalah about the situation, about my son's progress in some areas, and lack of progress in others. He wasn't failing anymore, but he was dangerously close to getting a D in two of his classes. His attitude toward school had changed a little, but in addition to all the other problems, I could see boredom setting in. He didn't want to go to school. Getting him out of bed required an appointment with a jackhammer — not to mention a pogo stick, an insurance waiver, and an act of God to get into his cluttered room.

Sesvalah told me, "There are some children that don't necessarily do well in the traditional school environment. You should try him in a charter school or an alternative school."

I had heard students in some charter schools were outperforming students in public schools located in the same areas. Unfortunately, the waiting list for the charter school in our area was so long that my son wouldn't get in until it was time to graduate.

At first I balked at the idea of an alternative school; I didn't like the label that came with it. Most people believe that alternative schools are for dropouts, or students with learning disabilities. The alternative school close to us seemed nice, but I had judged the place before I had even set foot in the building. I was ready, once again, to ship my son off to Job Corps or military school — anything but an alternative school.

As it turned out, I had no choice but to put him in the alternative school; other public schools wouldn't take some of his private school credits and he would have to repeat some subjects. I had a heck of a time trying to get him to pass those classes the first time. No way would I be able to convince him to re-take classes.

I enrolled him in the school. Not only did his grades soar, but his attitude toward school did a 360-degree turn. I no longer had to wake him up for school — he was up before me and out the door! The teachers were experienced and dedicated, and it showed in the type of work my son brought home. I now had to make an appointment to use my own computer! My son wanted every assignment to be presented in its best form — the way my son once took pride in his work was back. When I looked at some of those assignments I realized that the work was harder than at any of the schools he attended previously.

One day I asked him what was so different about the new school. He said, "They teach us like we can learn. They haven't already decided that we can't."

The teachers' attitude inspires the students and more than eighty percent of the students from that school are accepted and attend colleges and universities nationwide. I'm proud to say that my son was one of them. Halfway through his first year, he had offers from four different universities, one of them in the top ten. He is now a sophomore at the university of his choosing. It shows that the Creator will give us our heart's desire, regardless of what things seem like; regardless of ACT scores, SAT scores or other restrictions.

*S*peaking it into Existence:

When presented with a problem and we're unsure of what to do, we should always seek the wisdom of the Creator. We need to take the time to pray and meditate and then just begin to give thanks for answered prayers.

Example: "Thank you God for (fill in your desire), or better. And so it is."

*P*ersonal recipe

Pull out your personal journal or the Speak it into Existence journal. Take a moment to jot down information that came to mind as you read this chapter. Then write down your own formula for speaking it into existence. It can be an affirmation, Bible verse, mantra, etc., but it should be something that you'll use everyday until you see your desire come into existence.

MARTINA

CHALLENGE: FOLLOWING HER INNER SPIRIT/FORGIVENESS
AGE: **40**
STATUS: **SINGLE MOTHER**
OCCUPATION: **LEGAL SECRETARY**
SPIRITUAL BACKGROUND: **BAPTIST**

Working a second job and caring for my son meant, I had a lot going on in my life. Ultimately, this affected my ability to get a good night's sleep. After a week of only four hours of sleep per night, I was in a rare mood — a crazy kind of mood. I became very quiet and it didn't take much to irritate me. My boss, Helen, was pregnant. She wasn't dealing well with her raging hormones and sometimes she took it out on me. She would make smart little comments that would make me sad or feel inadequate.

Things got to the point I stopped making small talk with her and kept to myself. I did exactly as she asked, after writing it down so she couldn't say that she'd said something else — a common problem. Some days it even got so bad that I didn't want to come in to work. I kept telling myself, "She's pregnant. It'll pass." But I think it was more than that. Being pregnant is a wonderful thing; I've been through it once and it didn't change my personality or the way I treated people.

Just at the point I was ready to go to human resources and ask for a transfer, my other boss called me into his office and told me that Helen had a talk with human resources. A talk that had them coming to him asking about my performance. He asked me what was going on. I told him a little bit about what was going on in my life.

"Why didn't you tell me? You need a day off! Two days off. No wonder you haven't been your talkative self. I thought I had done something wrong."

"No, you're good people. I'll get some rest."

"Take Friday and Monday off. No writing, no television, just relaxing. That's a prescription."

"Are you going to bill me for that?"

"I'm a lawyer," he said, smiling and shooing me out of the office. "I bill for everything."

I felt a little better as I sat at my desk. Then Sharon, the human resources director, Sharon, called me in for a "talk." After all that I put up with from her, Helen had the nerve to complain about me. I was pissed — although I will say in Helen's defense, that I hadn't been as attentive as normal and had been a little distracted at times since I had so much going on.

Sharon told me, "Well she feels that you're a little . . . short with her."

Me? Short with her?

"And that you're not giving your all these days."

Hello! No one feels like giving a hundred and fifty percent when it's not appreciated.

"If you hadn't showed her what you could do in the beginning, she wouldn't expect so much. You were like a steamroller — it made the other secretaries a little jealous."

Well what could I say to that? "You know, before you called," I said, "I had planned to come down here to request a transfer."

The woman sighed and sat back in her chair. "There's nowhere to put you right now. There are no new people coming in; everyone else seems to be happy where they are . . ."

She smiled sweetly. I got the message: everyone was happy 'cept little ol' me.

"She's only going to be here for three more weeks," Sharon said. "See if you can tough it out. Just tell her you'll do what it takes to get her through the next weeks. Tell her you're back on board."

Back on board, what the heck is that?

"You can do it, I have faith in you." *The good old pep talk, laced with the kind of stuff that fills Pampers.*

I went back to my desk feeling real low and a little angry. How dare this heifer go to human resources! I'd never had that happen before. I began to weigh my options: stick out the three weeks or find another job. With the economy on the blink, finding another job would not be as easy as it had been in the past.

Two hours later I thought I had calmed down, so I got up from my desk, walked toward Helen's door, plastered a smile on my face, and went into her office. "Do you have a minute?"

She looked up and both of us bristled at my caustic tone. *Where did it come from?* I thought my anger had subsided. It hadn't. I should have excused myself and gone back to my desk right then. But I didn't. She slowly placed the folders she held into her out tray and said uncertainly, "Sure. Come on in."

What happened next could only be termed what Black women call a "come to Jesus meeting," where you tell a person off or set them straight. I glared at Helen, barely holding in the anger I thought I didn't have. "I will do whatever it takes to get you to March 14th. You ARE leaving on March 14th aren't you?" When Sharon said those words, they sounded like business; when I repeated them they sounded downright ugly.

She winced and said in a cautious tone, "Yeah, I think so."

"Well, I just had a talk with Sharon and she explained your concerns. I just wanted to let you know that I'm back on board and will see you out the door."

Did I sound like I wanted the woman and her hormones to leave? You bet! I KNEW I was being wrong and did nothing to curb it.

"Don't you think we should talk about this a little more?"

"Is there something you'd like to say besides the things you mentioned to human resources? I mean, Sharon was very clear on your complaints."

She looked a little sheepish and her lips twisted in a slight grimace. "Well,

I normally wouldn't go to them in the first place, but you've seemed so . . . unapproachable these days. I thought I needed someone to get your attention."

"Understood." I snapped. "Is there anything else?"

"No," she stammered and looked a little lost.

The truth was, I was insubordinate and I knew it. She could've had me rolled out of there in a Chicago second but I didn't care. And I should have. (It was close to that time of the month, but that couldn't be the only reason for my anger.) Lack of sleep couldn't be used to justify my behavior either. I felt a large rubber stamp aiming at my forehead, one with a label on it that began with the letter b and ended with the letter h.

No matter how my boss had been treating me, I had no right to treat her that way. Spiritually, I knew better.

She lowered her eyes and when she looked back at me she said, "I'm sorry you feel that way. I guess we'll get through the next weeks."

The truth be told, my male boss outranked her. I was cool with him, and knew that she couldn't have me bounced from my job without him having something to say. I still should have known better.

When I left Helen's office, I stopped at the door and looked back at her.

She immediately grabbed her coat and ran — not wobbled — out of there. I didn't even sit all the way down at my desk before a pain stabbed me in the chest. I thought I was having a heart attack. Some say that what goes around, comes around. Well, that happens a lot faster for those who are supposed to spiritually aware. I hadn't been too spiritual that morning and the only thing I was aware of was that I had been wrong, yet didn't walk away to get my act together.

I began to walk slowly down the long hallway, in the opposite direction my boss had gone. My mind was on the commercial that says, "When you feel an attack coming on, take some aspirin." Well, the aspirin was a long way from my desk — all the way at reception, almost two miles away — at least is seemed that way at the time.

As I inched my way to reception, the pain would come and go. I didn't want to run and aggravate my heart. My mother had died from a heart attack a year before and that was foremost on my mind as the pain kept coming. Finally, one of my co-workers appeared in the long hallway. Something made me ask, "Hey, what side is the heart on?"

He pointed to the left side of his body. I breathed a small sigh of relief. The pain was on the right side of my chest. No heart attack. I still kept going toward the aspirin just in case. I took two and went back to my desk to think over what I'd done. The physical pain was just a sign, my body's way of saying, "See, you know better than that!"

The pain began to subside, but only a little. Emotionally, I felt low. I should not have said the things I said and the way I said them. I sat at the desk and didn't move. I knew that when Helen came back, I would have to handle things better.

As the pain continued to lessen, I started packing my things, because I knew that my actions had probably gotten me fired. There was no excuse for what I did and even if he could have, I didn't want my male boss to save me on this one. I prepared to pay the ultimate price — the loss of a good job.

Helen strolled back sixty-seven minutes later. I gave her a few moments to hang up her coat and get settled. Then I walked in her office and said, in a much gentler tone and spirit than I had earlier, "Do you have a minute?"

She looked up. Her eyes were so red that I felt like a sledgehammer had just slammed into my stomach. "Helen, I apologize for the way I spoke to you and for how I acted. I never meant to hurt you. I was angry and should never have said a word to you that way."

She got out of her chair and she hugged me. She actually hugged me. And then she said something that made my mouth fall open.

"Martina, I'm sorry I even went to human resources. You had a right to be angry—"

"But I didn't have a right to take it out on you that way and I truly apologize."

"You know, I don't think it was your words or your tone that got to me."

I frowned because I couldn't think of what else would.

"I don't think you even realize it, but on your way out the door you did a little curtsy." She shook her head vehemently as if trying to shake the memory.

"I couldn't believe it. It was like something out of the Deep South or like you were a servant or something. I . . .I couldn't believe it."

"I don't even remember doing it."

"Oh, you did. And if at any time I've ever made you feel like a servant, I'm so sorry. I never . . . I never . . ."

She almost broke out in tears again.

We hugged like we were sisters or even old friends.

My chest still hurt, and I realized that the physical sign of being "less than the spiritual" me would take a while to go away completely.

"Please forgive me for not being sensitive to your situation."

She looked up and blinked.

"No, I don't mean just the pregnancy. I mean the fact that you've had twice as much work thrown at you lately, and that at every turn they're trying to remind you that as a woman with a family on the way you don't measure up like the fellas."

"I didn't think you understood that."

"I've seen it at almost every job I've had. It's like a mission for them to make sure women know that the men can do their jobs and not have a family interrupt things. But then again, if men were having the babies, there'd be a lot less of them."

She chuckled as she followed me back to my desk. She saw my bags and my desk cleared. "Where are you going?"

"I thought that I was out of a job."

She grimaced. "I wouldn't have done that."

"I wasn't so sure."

"Well, it's water under the bridge."

Our relationship improved. Helen was mindful of her words and how she treated me. I felt much better after a two-day rest and was truly "back on board again" and not just with my job, but on listening to that still, small voice before I allowed my emotions to dominate a situation.

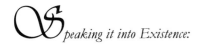

Speaking it into Existence:

Once we say: "I'm going to see the Christ Consciousness in everyone I meet," does that mean we're going to let someone abuse us? No. Just because that person won't let the Christ in them come out, we should not emulate the negative behavior. It's during that time that we'll be tested. We should keep in mind: "I don't care how this person acts, based on where I am I'm staying in the consciousness of who God is and I will salute the God in everyone."

As we encounter challenging situations, we should say, "God be with me in this meeting when I speak to my boss, (or teacher, or co-worker). Let me speak with the knowledge of who God is." If we keep that as our focus, then we will be mindful of our words and our actions.

If dissension comes in when we're feeling a little low, if it disrupts relationships or causes discord to get us off target, we must keep our eye on the prize, and begin to see the Christ Consciousness in everything that happens. Before we open our mouths, we should ask, "Am I allowing God to speak through me? Or am I allowing the little ego to edge God out and to speak through me?"

Once again, I will say: Words have power. Thoughts have power. What kind of power and energy are we giving to our spoken words? And do we really want our spoken words to manifest in someone else's life — or our own?

Personal recipe

Pull out your personal journal or the Speak it into Existence journal. Take a moment to jot down information that came to mind as you read this chapter. Then write down your own formula for speaking it into existence. It can be an affirmation, Bible verse, mantra, etc., but it should be something that you'll use everyday until you see your desire come into existence.

When we want to attract something different or new, we have to let go of the old — clean out our refrigerator, give away our old clothes, change our attitude about ourselves or others. Change — Change — Change. As we are doing this we need to say: I release all worn-out conditions, thoughts, situations, and things in my life. I release, anger, pain, etc. and I accept love, peace — my new car, house, (or whatever you desire).

ANDREA

CHALLENGE: **NEEDS A PIANO FOR HER SON**

AGE: **36**

STATUS: **SINGLE MOTHER**

OCCUPATION: **GRAPHIC DESIGNER**

SPIRITUAL BACKGROUND: **A.M.E.**

When my son was six years old, I enrolled him in a piano class. After the first few classes it dawned on me that he needed to practice on a regular basis. This created somewhat of a problem since we didn't own, or have access to, a piano.

I begin to declare and thank God for my piano, *at little or no cost to me.* I continued to give thanks with expectation of the fulfillment of my desire. I would share with others that I was expecting a piano for my son, at little or no cost to me.

A few weeks later, the music director at my church told me that he was purchasing a new piano and that I could have his current one. It would only cost me $50 to have it moved from his house to mine.

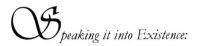

Speaking it into Existence:

The power of the spoken word, whether it is positive or negative, brings forth whatever it is we put into the universe. As we know that energy follows thought, so will the actions that are stirred be manifested by your words.

Jesus said to the lame man lying by the pool, "Rise, take up thy bed and walk." We must take up our own bed and walk. We must perform some action that shows that we are preparing for our goal.

For example, a person might say, "I want to go back to school." The school doesn't come to the house, walk through the door, and begin classes.. That person has to research the school that offers the type of classes he/she wants, e time within their schedule, etc.

As we pray to God, the Creator, we set our goals, and contemplate our desires. It takes our belief joined with some type of physical action to bring about good results.

ersonal recipe —————————————————————————————————

Pull out your personal journal or the Speak it into Existence journal. Take a moment to jot down information that came to mind as you read this chapter. Then write down your own formula for speaking it into existence. It can be an affirmation, Bible verse, mantra, etc., but it should be something that you'll use everyday until you see your desire come into existence.

Cassondra

CHALLENGE: NEW HOUSE (WITH NO CREDIT, NO SOURCE OF INCOME)

AGE: **19**

STATUS: **SINGLE MOTHER**

OCCUPATION: **STAY-AT-HOME MOTHER**

SPIRITUAL BACKGROUND: **SOUTHERN BAPTIST**

Cassondra lived with her mother, but after her son was born she wanted her own place. Living with Mom was good, but Cassondra wanted her independence.

She began to buy dishes, silverware, sheets, and other items for the new house she didn't have. She didn't know where it would be. She didn't even have a job and couldn't start looking for one until the baby was at least six weeks old.

She continued to plan for her new place. She received some financial assistance, and although most of the funds went to her mother, she saved the rest. She didn't want an apartment — she'd always liked the spaciousness of a house. But at the rate she was going, and with the tiny amount she had saved she'd never have a house. Even though things seemed challenging, Cassondra kept purchasing a few new things and putting them under the baby's crib.

One day Sharon, a childhood friend who lived down the street, told Cassondra that her family was having financial trouble and would be moving soon. She told Cassondra she could move in for a little while and save more money. Several weeks later, Sharon called and told Cassandra the coast was clear. After they moved out, but just before the house was to be boarded up, Cassondra walked into the now-vacant house, then had a friend change the locks.

The next day Cassondra sat in Com Ed's office with her son bouncing on her left knee as she explained that she needed the service turned on in her name. Next she took the electric company's receipt to the gas company and they turned the service on in her name. Those receipts were enough to get telephone service.

Cassondra cleaned the house and had a neighbor move her bed and other furniture from her mother's house. She moved her smaller personal items.

The whole block thought she'd lost her mind. Even her mother said, "Girl, you're crazy. They're gonna put you out of there."

Cassondra hadn't lost it; she was testing out an old theory — Homesteading or Squatter's Rights. As long as she maintained the property, the legal owners — in this case the mortgage company — had to offer it to her before anyone else. At least she hoped it still worked that way.

Cassondra stayed in the house, rent free, for close to a year before the Veteran's Administration came to her door informing her they owned the property. Cassondra gave them copies of her bills showing she had been there all year and receipts for repairs she'd made.

After a few days, she was given clearance to purchase the house. Grateful she'd had a year to raise her son, Cassondra got a job with the City of Chicago. Unfortunately, her salary wasn't enough to get the house. She signed up to sell Avon and that made the difference. It didn't hurt that the loan officer really wanted her to have the house.

Cassondra had high school students sell boxes of candy to help her raise the rest of the large down payment.

She bought the house. She still ate at her mom's house three doors down but slept in her own home. Cassondra thought it was the perfect arrangement!

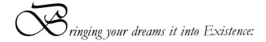

Bringing your dreams it into Existence:

After we have prayed or affirmed our desires, we need to thank the Creator and write down our goals. We must do some physical action to impress on our consciousness that we are working in faith, knowing that a way will be made. We can purchase glasses to be used only at our new house — a mail box, or something that is only to be used when the deal has been closed and we have the key.

Always speak in the *now*. We need to speak the solution we desire and not the problem. Thank you lord that I am healed, or that I have peace of mind. Dwell on the solution; if we focus on the problem we'll have MORE of the problem.

The spoken word creates our world. Remember that the Bible says, "And whatsoever ye shall ask in my name, that will I do, that the father may be glorified in the son."

Affirmation:

"I thank the Creator, my source, for the perfect home at the perfect place, in the perfect way — right now — and so it is."

Personal recipe

Pull out your personal journal or the Speak it into Existence journal. Take a moment to jot down information that came to mind as you read this chapter. Then write down your own formula for speaking it into existence. It can be an affirmation, Bible verse, mantra, etc., but it should be something that you'll use everyday until you see your desire come into existence.

The words we speak bring life or death into our lives. We want life, abundance, joy, peace, and harmony in who we are. We want those things in our lives, and in the lives of the people around us. We have to remember that in every apparent challenge or situation we're being transformed and that our minds are being renewed because we're staying in the Christ Consciousness, which means we're keeping our consciousness on God and only God.

ROMULUS

CHALLENGE: **NEW JOB**

AGE: **57**

STATUS: **SINGLE**

OCCUPATION: **TEACHER**

SPIRITUAL BACKGROUND: **BUDDHIST**

Following an unsuccessful business venture, Rom needed to generate more income. He began by being more consistent with his prayers and meditations, then he went out and applied for six jobs.

Rom received five calls and went on the interviews. He held out for the job he wanted most. They finally made an offer he accepted — truly a blessing to everyone involved.

While his new job was wonderful, his supervisor had a much-deserved reputation for being cantankerous. Her manner was brutal; her verbal style was both volatile and sarcastic. Rom had not been on the job very long before he witnessed her verbally brutalize and denigrate every single one of his co-workers. Rom knew his time would come; the woman spared no one.

Rom decided that he needed to purposely and persistently project divine and unconditional love toward her every day. His intention was, and continued to be, to radiate that love to every aspect of her being.

As a result, he observed a dramatic shift in his supervisor's demeanor and approach. She became a kinder and gentler being who demonstrated fairness, compassion, and moderation with her staff, clients, and constituents.

The atmosphere in the office became one of cooperation and tranquility and continues to be that way even though his supervisor has moved to another position and another one replaced her.

Rom didn't change her, he changed *himself* and how he reacted to her. He practiced the principles of unconditional love. The two most important commandments are to love God first then to love our neighbor as ourselves. All the great prophets in some way, expounded on this belief.

We should be diligent in the pursuit of our goals and dreams. Put the Creator first in our lives, then loving our neighbor should not be such a hardship — even though some of our neighbors, family, and friends can really test our spiritual belief system.

Sometimes Romulus made a decision to do both. In prayer and supplication to God, he sought the presence of the Lord to lead, guide, and direct him. He followed the still small voice, and his prayers were answered. He practiced the Universal Principles and everyone around him was blessed by his prayers and expressions of unconditional love.

ersonal recipe

Pull out your personal journal or the Speak it into Existence journal. Take a moment to jot down information that came to mind as you read this chapter. Then write down your own formula for speaking it into existence. It can be an affirmation, Bible verse, mantra, etc., but it should be something that you'll use everyday until you see your desire come into existence.

MINDY

CHALLENGE: NEW JOB
AGE: **36**
STATUS: **SINGLE MOTHER**
OCCUPATION: **GRAPHIC DESIGNER**
SPIRITUAL BACKGROUND: **CATHOLIC**

I needed a new job in a different field. I had been fired when I started my singing career and couldn't work overtime anymore. But working at a club a few nights a week didn't pay my serious bills — like rent, gas, light and telephone.

I signed up with a temp agency and a few good nibbles came my way, but only for three- or six-month stints. One day, the agency called and asked me to go on an interview for a job that required several years of experience in the legal field. I only had about three total, and not all in the same firm, so I didn't expect to get the job.

I went on the interview anyway but didn't feel confident that I'd get the job, especially knowing their requirements. I met with both of the people who would be my bosses if they accepted me for the job. I was very comfortable with them and thought, *They would be excellent people to work with.* One was a family man, who made sure he went home to tuck his sons in every night. The other was a woman who had just gotten married a month before — she was still in the honeymoon stage.

I left the place and didn't think any more about the job. A week later, the agency called me and told me the law firm offered me the job.

"Me?" I asked dumbly.

"Is there anyone else on the phone?" the woman asked.

"Well, you know I do hear voices . . ."

"Very funny," she said. "They're offering about $3,000 more than the last place you worked."

"When do I start?"

I've been with the firm for almost two years and because of my schedule, I'm also able to pursue my dream.

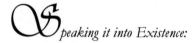 *peaking it into Existence:*

Thank the Creator that "riches in glory are unlimited, without restriction, continuously replenishing itself right here on earth. That the Universe gives us an unlimited reservoir that is always there."

How do we tap into that unlimited resource? We begin by activating our seed of faith — the seed that was planted in each one of us. Nourish that seed, water it with positive energy and affirmative thought, and watch what blooms.

We must establish faith in the omnipresence of God as our supply. Continue to say, "God is my supply." Decide on the type of job we want. Write it out, then prepare for the job — buy a new business suit, if that is what's required for the job or buy a new lunch box; something to claim the new job.

Speak: "The Creator shall lead me to my perfect position with the perfect boss, perfect coworkers in peace and harmony. My word shall not return void to me."

We want to develop an affirmation, Bible verse or mantra that we can remember and say often.

Proverbs tells us: "A man shall be satisfied with good by the fruits of his mouth." We must bring forth our fruit and speak the words that create and nourish that fruit.

ersonal recipe

Pull out your personal journal or the Speak it into Existence journal.
Take a moment to jot down information that came to mind as you read this
chapter. Then write down your own formula for speaking it into existence. It
can be an affirmation, Bible verse, mantra, etc., but it should be something
that you'll use everyday until you see your desire come into existence.

The Creator, in the Divine Plan, brings circumstances that not only test our faith and desire — but confirm that we are working in Divine Order.

MAYA

CHALLENGE: OVERCOMING SEXUAL ABUSE/CHILD ABUSE
AGE: **36**
STATUS: **SINGLE MOTHER**
OCCUPATION: **LAWYER**
SPIRITUAL BACKGROUND: BAPTIST

Note: This story and personal revelation, used by permission, is combined from a series of counseling sessions with one of my members. The woman, co-author of this book (Naleighna Kai), was in counseling with me for weeks before she was able to tell the full story. She has since written *She Touched My Soul,* a novel built on this story. She has also written several other books to help women heal from incest and other forms of abuse.

Names, locations, and the sequence of events have been changed to protect the innocent, but the experiences and emotional impact are told the way they happened to Maya, the character in the novel. Here's her story.

I don't remember a lot about my early years. The only person in my biological family I have contact with is my brother. I remember when I was seven, I realized I was treated differently. Sometimes just the sight of me was enough to make my mother angry. I became very familiar with extension cords, hangers, brooms, belts, shoes or whatever else she could get reach.

When my mother finally found traditional religion, she found justification for her acts. "Spare the rod, spoil the child," made an unpleasant situation even worse. I wasn't a bad child. I couldn't understand why it was happening to me. I didn't have to do anything wrong; no matter what I did — sit, stand, smile, or lie still — it was the wrong thing.

School became my escape. I excelled in my studies because I liked school. Actually, I liked any place that wasn't home. No one believed how mean my mother could be. Anyone who didn't live in our house never knew the truth. She treated strangers better than me. I never knew why it was only me she vented on. Maybe it was because I had a different father than my sister and brother.

My brother would sometimes stop my mom — he was successful only half of the time but even for that I was grateful. My sister didn't care one way or the other. When my brother left for good, there was no one to speak for me. I missed him so much.

When I was fourteen, things got so bad I decided it would be better to live with a father I barely knew. He sometimes came to my mother's house bearing money and gifts. He never laid a hand on me or mistreated me. I saw him as a sort like Santa Claus. When the school year ended, my father welcomed me in his home. For a while things were fine. But after living in close quarters for a short period of time, he stopped seeing me as his daughter.

At fourteen, my body started attracting a lot of unwanted male attention. I didn't understand how the addition of a few curves could change how people looked at me — how they thought of me.

One day my father moved all of his belongings into the other apartment he owned next door and informed me of my new station in life: I was to be an in-house source for sex. He forced me to bed and tried to have sex with me. My struggles turned him off — at first. He would repeat the process every day, several times a day. He would be aroused at first but my struggles would put him off. He wanted me to give in, and when I wouldn't, he couldn't go on. Fighting was my only weapon.

It would have been so much easier to just give him what he wanted, but my body and mind rebelled at the thought. At times, I wanted to give up. Maybe if I did that, it would end things, and I would be free in some way.

He used my nightgown to tie me to the bed and gag me. My father stopped going out for anything but work. At strange times of the day, he would come in and check to see if I was ready to give in. Most of the time he would come after I fell deep asleep. I'd wake to find him using my nightclothes to suffocate me, pulling them over my head so I couldn't see. Clothes became restrictive for me, because he used them any number of ways to restrain or disorient me. Many times I would wake up with him on top trying to get inside me.

After several weeks, when he failed to get results, he decided to use another method. In order to get food or trips to the chamber, I was given the option of having sex with him or getting a whipping. I chose the whippings because I was used to them. My screams would probably have woken the entire building if I hadn't been gagged. The silence on the outside didn't lessen the scream inside of my head. My father got off on it, enjoying every minute.

One day he was frustrated and decided to just beat me so I would weaken. In his frustration at still not being successful, he made the mistake of untying both my hands and feet — possibly attempting another way around his problem.

We lived on the third floor, but there was a big picture window in the center of the living room. I bolted through the window, ready to run for my life — landing soundly on the walkway. I must have finally caught a lucky break because I wasn't seriously injured — lots of cuts, but no broken bones.

Two women were sitting on the porch and saw me land. They gathered me up and took me into their home. They wanted to call the police, but I wouldn't let them. My father was the police. His dark blue uniform and badge were firmly etched in my memory. That's how I knew it was him walking up the driveway to visit me at my mother's home. The uniform and the badge used to be a sign of good things. Amazing how the actions of the person behind it can change the meaning of something. He told me no one would believe a runaway child over a police officer. I wasn't sure what they would believe, so I didn't take the chance.

I didn't know it then, but had I let the ladies call the police, his friends on the force would have become his instant enemies. Cops don't play when it comes to that sort of thing. They would have beaten my father without mercy. But I didn't know that. Instead, the women called my mother.

I stayed with her until I was sixteen. When I couldn't take it any longer, I moved in with Cheryl. Up until then, she had been one of my mother's friends.

She had watched me grow up. She was married and had four teenage boys and a toddler. I settled into a new house and pretty much stayed to myself and out of everyone's way.

SESVALAH'S NOTE:

There is a great deal more to this story, but for brevity's sake, I will state that after counseling, Maya was able to begin to heal from her experiences, and it has been a daily process even after the end of counseling.

As I tell so many women who come to me: The counseling process is to help find answers. Some people find their answers right away, and for some it's a longer process, taking weeks or months to bring about a change. People may have already made some healing milestones on their own, but talking with someone can make all the difference in the world. Incest, childhood abuse or rape issues are especially hard to work through because women sometimes have a tendency to get up, dust themselves off, and walk away — or bury it so deep they can't remember what happened.

While healing. a person can take ten steps forward, then a memory, or something as small as a smell, or seeing a person or thing, can trigger a reaction that makes a person take two or three steps back. During the healing process, the person becomes stronger with each step so each setback doesn't necessarily mean that he/she will go back to the depths they once were.

In the next few pages, Maya continues to share her healing process. With the support of her friend Mykal, Myaa confronts her mother in an effort to understand the root cause of her abuse. In the process she learns that her mother is also carrying a dark secret.

MAYA PART II
CHALLENGE: FORGIVENESS

Maya grew up in a place called Jeffrey Manor, a section of Chicago filled with town houses, duplexes, winding streets, and horseshoe-shaped blocks. From the air the area looks like the Jewish menorah — the nine candlesticks.

Maya drove up to a green and white, nicely kept brick house on Merrion Avenue. The small flower garden and dark green manicured lawn out front gave it a warm, welcoming feel.

Maya didn't think that it was so welcoming. She sat in the car so long her friend, Mykal thought she would change her mind. Holding her hand, he started saying a prayer for her and her mother, hoping the visit would provide the answers that Maya needed.

After they prayed, Maya got out of the car and scanned the area before walking up the driveway. She took a deep breath and rang the bell.

"Who's there?" A woman asked.

"Maya Gervais."

"Who?"

Maya winced, blinking. After a short pause, "I mean, Maya Anderson. Your daughter." Maya had changed her name and lived in hiding for years, praying that her father wouldn't find her. She hadn't seen her mother in seventeen years.

The door swung open. A small, older version of Maya peered at them. Her hair was pulled back neatly in a bun and her clothes — a casual pantsuit, white ruffled blouse — were very conservative. It was obvious where Maya got her taste in clothes. The woman's eyes were those of one who had seen plenty and lived to tell about it. Her gaze traveled over Maya, eyes alight with appreciation. Her eyes glazed over with tears before she looked away. She finally said, "Come in, child."

"Mother, this is my friend Mykal."

"Hello, Ms. Anderson."

She nodded, shaking his extended hand, while she peered at him through suspicious eyes.

Mother escorted us into her living room. "What brings you here, Maya? I never expected you to come again."

"I never expected to see you again either."

"So why did you come?"

Maya's voice was strong and sure. "To understand. To ask…why?"

"Why?"

"Yes, why did you hate me so much? Why did you treat me the way you did? What did I ever do to cause you to hate me so much? There has to be a reason."

She grimaced, remained silent for a few moments, and then nodded at my friend. "Who's this young man?"

Maya held his hand firmly in hers. "He's someone that's been very good to me and I love him." (Actually, Mykal, an R&B singer, had fallen in love with Maya and had done everything possible to change her life and bring her to a point where she could heal.)

Maya's mother glanced around the warm, cozy living room, before allowing her dark brown, almond-shaped eyes to rest on Maya. "So you understand what love is?"

"I'm learning day by day."

"I'm glad you are. Your father certainly didn't." A few moments later she asked, "Are you sure you want to hear what I have to say? It's not something I've shared before, but if it'll help you in some way, I'll tell you."

"Yes. I want to hear what happened. It's probably better than what I've been thinking all these years. I have to know."

Maya's mother sat still for several minutes. Her blinking was the only thing that signaled any signs of life. She finally took a deep breath and began: "Your father did things to me that are still unmentionable. Things I never knew could be done to a woman. It didn't start out that way. I was taking a cab to work and had an epileptic seizure. The driver panicked and instead of taking me to the hospital, he flagged the nearest police officer. Your father. He took me to the hospital and stayed there with me all day.

He was very kind to me, and we eventually started dating. I already had two children, and that usually scared men off. He made sure that I wanted for nothing, and I was very grateful to him. Even after dating for a time, something about him still made me hold back. When I tried to break it off, things went to hell. When I refused to have sex with him — he turned . . . evil."

She grimaced, crossing her legs under her. "Then the sex wasn't just with him. He would invite some of his fellow officers here. When I tried to break it off with him or refused, he threatened to have me arrested and thrown in jail. He said then the real fun would begin because the whole force would get to me, not just the friends that he brought by from time to time. I believed he could make good on his threat. The fact that his friends not only turned a blind eye, but participated in what he did, convinced me. "

Glancing into the curio cabinet, her gaze fell on the jade, stone, and wood elephants inside. "I went to another district very far away from the one he worked in and filed a complaint. It got back to him and he beat the hell out of me. I never tried again. He had too many friends on the force. In addition to the beatings, he threatened he would take your sister for his own use if I ever did anything like that again. After that threat, I sent your sister and brother to stay with their father for their own protection. The fear, the sexual assaults, and the beatings went on for years. When the others tired of me, he still kept coming."

Maya's eyes filled with compassion, glazing over with tears that wouldn't fall. "Mama, how did you get away from him?"

She looked at the ceiling and then back at Maya. "One day I was just tired of it and decided that I didn't want to live. I took some pills just before he came over and they took effect while he was on me. I thought my last conscious moments on earth would be getting free of him."

"I stopped breathing and was on my way to freedom. He must have reacted right away, because the next thing I can remember is that I was in the hospital."

She cleared her throat. "After I left the hospital, I found out that I was pregnant with his child. It was too early for the hospital tests to show it. I was ashamed I got pregnant by him. His visits didn't always allow me time to set up prevention. I knew it was his child because the other men always used condoms. He was the only one who didn't."

She shivered, but continued in a monotone, "I tried everything in my power to end the pregnancy. Old household remedies like large doses of quinine sulfate, liquor, falling down the stairs, strenuous lifting. None of them worked. Just as determined as I was to be rid of the child, the child was determined to be here." Maya winced. Mykal tightened his hand on hers as Maya's mother continued. "I finally resigned myself to the fact that I would have a constant reminder of him." Her gaze fell to Maya. "I know it's unfair, but because of him, I hated you before you were even born. I know that's not an excuse for what I did but it's the only one I have."

Maya's low voice dripped with contempt. "Why didn't you just give me up for adoption? Why did you keep me?"

Her mother crooked her mouth into something that wasn't quite a smile. "I did give you away at birth. I signed into the hospital under my sister's name — Patricia Fields." She sighed. "When I left the hospital my sister was there to take you off my hands and see to your upbringing. Your aunt couldn't have any children, so the arrangement worked out fine. I didn't see you again until eighteen months later when Pat went to Mississippi to meet the parents of her new husband. You were too sick to travel and they couldn't postpone the trip again. She asked me to keep you for a week. I agreed.

"While she was there her husband was shot and killed by a man who had a problem with what he called, 'well-dressed, educated niggers.' Pat's husband went into a store to buy some things and when the owner shorted him several dollars on his change, her husband pointed it out. The argument turned fatal, and the store owner shot him. Pat picked up a hammer and laid into the man's head while the gun was still smoking. I'm not sure if it was stupidity or love, but Pat killed the man and was sent to prison. Pat always had a hard streak." She smiled and shook her head. "The softest I've ever seen her nature was when she had you. She loved you so, so very much."

Maya's mother stood, opened the draperies, and let in a little more sunlight.

"Her actions meant that I was stuck with you — again." Taking a long, slow breath, she continued. "A month later, I was still trying to figure out what to do with you when things changed again. I was at work and my neighbor was supposed to be watching you. You accidentally swallowed some cleaning solution and had to be taken to the emergency room. You stayed in the hospital for a few weeks. During that time I had to go through the process of adopting you, becoming your guardian — the only way for you to receive medical treatment or for me to see about your welfare. I had to tell the court that I lied on the birth certificate."

Maya leaned forward, her gaze locked on her mother's as she sat down once again. "Why see about me at all, Mama? Why not just let me become a ward of the state?"

She shrugged, her thin lips etched with a bitter smile. "Maya, I didn't think like that then. I didn't want you to die. You were still my child. My responsibility. You drank enough of the chemicals that it should have taken you out of here. But you were a strong one then. Judging by the looks of things, you're even stronger now." Maya's mother actually sounded proud of Maya.

She lowered her eyes, then looked up at Maya. "I'm not going to lie and say that I felt anything motherly toward you, because I didn't. You were your father's child, and every time I saw you, I saw my own weakness and stupidity. I didn't understand that in hurting you, I was really trying to hurt him. I know that's not something that will sit well with you, but that's how it seems to me now."

Maya scooted to the edge of the sofa. "Mama, what happened when you left the hospital?"

Her mother bit her bottom lip and looked at the plush cream carpet. "He stopped coming by, but he had his boys ride past the house or the place I worked sometimes to remind me to keep my mouth shut. When he found out I was pregnant he started coming by again. He forced me to have sex with him, and it wasn't as . . . sick as before. But it was only a matter of time. I found that if I pretended to enjoy it, it was normal sex. If I refused, he turned evil. He had a serious problem with being rejected."

She stood, walked to the window, and placed her hands deep in her pockets. Noisy children played in her driveway. She smiled absently, then turned back to Maya. "When I gave you to Pat, I told him that you had died. I told him that there was nothing holding me here and that if he ever touched me again I would kill him. I should have. Giving him a warning like that was a big mistake."

"He immediately went to the phone and called someone. He said, 'take this address.' I was in shock when he gave the person the address of where your brother and sister were hiding. He added, 'If anything happens to me, fuck them both and kill them'."

Maya winced as her mother continued, "But he must have believed me because he stopped coming by — until you returned. Up until that point, I would pray for his death. But after the threat to your brother and sister, I prayed for him to live. If he died — even in the line of duty — my other children would be abused and killed."

"He found out the history and timing surrounding your birth and adoption and put two and two together."

"Why didn't you just leave? Take all of us somewhere?" Maya asked, squeezing Mykal's hand so tight it hurt. He patted Maya's hand gently. She released her grip a little.

Maya's mother laughed bitterly, spreading her slender hands. "Where would that be, Maya? No one was supposed to know where your brother and sister were. But he knew. If he could find them, then he could find us anywhere. How would I make a living? Put you in school? Provide for you? Where could I go?" Her body trembled, eyes glazed with tears. "Your father was a very powerful man. He would have found me. The only way to be rid of him would be my death or his. I couldn't die because he was the type to take revenge by using your sister or by using you. Females were just a receptacle for his lust — it didn't matter the age. I couldn't allow that to happen. I did try to go to the police in the next state, but because it was out of their jurisdiction, they couldn't help me.

"They referred me back to the Office of Professional Standards in Chicago.

I went there and filed a claim. They were ready to take action, but he found out and had someone take your sister; she was missing for hours. He personally brought her home — untouched — and didn't say a word. His message was clear. I never tried to get help again."

She sighed, sitting back down. "All this took a toll on my ability to work, and I went from job to job. Sometimes going for months with no income. He knew and he would come by and bring things for you from time to time and send money through others. I was always in fear that he could do something at any time. But he didn't touch me again."

She gazed at Maya. "When you ran away, I called the police and reported you missing. When you turned up at his home, they let it go. He told them that you were safe and he would take care of you. I knew I couldn't appeal to you to return home. There was nothing I could do to help you. My fear of him and my pain made me worse than him in a lot of ways. How could I reach you? I had no right to say that it would be better to be with me than with him. You had never known anything different. He had never threatened you at any time, only your sister. You were his own flesh and blood, maybe he would respect that."

Maya's hand tightened on Mykal's again. She glared furiously at her mother. "Did you really believe that, Mama?"

She shook her head. "But it's what I told myself anyway." She lowered her head. "When you returned three months later, you were . . . destroyed. Bruised, cut, bleeding and you had lost so much weight. You were close to death and the only part of you that seemed to have any life was your eyes. There was still a fire inside of them. Maybe you would fight and live." She shook her head. "I wasn't so sure."

She swallowed, holding in her tears. "When you came home from the hospital, you didn't speak to me again until you expressed a desire to go back to school. It was the only thing you asked me for — not clothes, not food, not even for bus fare. You walked to school no matter the distance or weather. You bartered your time at school for lunch or anything else you needed. You wouldn't ask me for anything."

Her eyes filled with tears. She sighed as she gazed at Maya. "The teachers constantly asked me what was going on. But I never told them. You did very well academically, but suffered socially. Other girls were jealous of your beauty, intelligence, and quietness. They picked on you constantly. A group cornered you in the bathroom and made the unfortunate mistake of touching you. Two were in the hospital for at least a week. But after that people left you alone."

She lowered her eyes to the folded hands resting on her lap. "Your brother and sister came home after you were released from the hospital. You would talk to them, but not to me. You were always so frustratingly polite, even when I did things to try to make up for the wrong I had done. I finally became so aggravated that I . . .slapped you. You didn't strike back, still feeling a certain level of respect for me that I didn't deserve."

She grimaced, smoothing her hair back. "You stood there silently, and when I was done you quietly went to your room and packed your things. I apologized to you. Your reply was that no matter what I said, it was the start of something old. You were tired of it. Once I started, I would not be able to stop. Your sister and brother were gone. You said that you would take your chances with strangers because family didn't give a damn. I haven't seen you since that day."

Tears streamed down Maya's face. She was having a hard time catching her breath. Mykal stroked her back and pulled her close. "Breathe, Maya. Breathe." Her body was so tense. "Breathe, Baby," he whispered softly.

Maya glanced at her mother, tears still flowing at a fast pace. "I was so prepared to hate you and to go on hating you, Mama."

Her mother nodded, holding her own tears in check. "You have every right to." She smiled grimly. "I think I hated myself more. At one time I had the chance and the strength to make things better and I didn't do anything. I blame no one but myself for what happened. I let fear of someone else rule my life, and allowed my maternal and survival instincts to die."

She reached for Maya, paused, then clasped her hands. Her dark brown eyes filled with sadness. "Maya, you were not responsible for what happened, but I blamed you. I used you, too. Hurting you was like hurting him. I have no right to ask your forgiveness, so I won't. I will say that I'm sorry I hurt you.

My punishment is that I will die old and alone."

She glanced around at her home. "Your sister and brother no longer come here. I have grandchildren I've never seen. My weakness cost me my family and I live with that fact every day. You're the first of my children who I've seen in more than fifteen years."

Maya held Mykal's hands, stroking them, trying to find comfort. "I will accept your apology, Mama, because I need to so I can move on. Hating you and my father has taken too much of my time and energy. It's time for me to move past this because it doesn't do me any good. There are so many beautiful things happening in my life right now and I can't enjoy them because I'm too filled with questions and pain." Her voice wavered. "But no more. It ends for me now. It ends today!"

Maya sniffed, trying unsuccessfully to remove the moisture from her face. "Mama, all these years, all I wanted you to do was love me." She shook her head briskly, tears flying in every direction. "I thought that if my own mother couldn't love me, no one else could. There's something not right about a mother not loving her child. I always thought that something was wrong with me." Maya pointed to her chest. "That I was so . . . ugly you . . . couldn't stand the sight of me. And everything that happened to me afterward seemed to prove that point."

For the first time, her mother cried.. She slowly raised her eyes to the ceiling. Her voice became soft. "I'm so sorry, Maya. Very truly sorry. I sit here sometimes and think about how different life would be if I had done this or that, but it wouldn't make a difference or change what actually happened. It wasn't you, Maya. It was never you."

Maya took a few moments to compose herself, before asking, "He never came back again?"

She shook her head. "Your doctor filed a police report based on your injuries; my testimony helped put your father in jail. When the story hit the papers more women came forward. There were a couple of women in jail that had something to say as well. Your father had them jailed under false charges. Their stories were even more bizarre than my own. Later, their convictions were overturned and they successfully sued the state for wrongful imprisonment. The money they received was nothing in comparison to all the time they spent behind bars.

"It frightened me to think that I could have been just like them. But in some ways, I was like them. I was in a prison, just one behind a different set of bars. You never had to testify, Maya. You wouldn't even if you had to. You were determined to finish school and leave my home." Her tear-filled eyes looked at Mykal, then to Maya. "You look well, Maya. I hope you did well for yourself. It's too late for me to do anything but think about what could have been but if you find a way, Maya, I hope you can find and truly experience love. I did once, so very long ago. I hope this young man will do right by you. You shouldn't end up like me — wishing life could have been different."

Maya embraced her. "You're wrong, Mama. There's always a time to heal. There's this woman I've been talking with. Her name is Sesvalah and maybe you should talk with her. I could set up a session for you."

Mykal's lips parted slightly, eyes wide with shock. Maya's mother winced, eyes equally wide. She cocked her head. "Why would you help me after everything I did to you?"

Maya sighed. "Mama, it doesn't cost me anything to help you. I'm letting it go. It's time you did the same. I forgive you, but I can't promise that I will become the dutiful daughter because I'm not sure that I have it in me. There's so much I'm working through right now and I can't say how I'll feel tomorrow, or the next day or the next week. It's a day-by-day process, but I'm healing." She took a deep breath. "I will promise you that you won't be alone. I know all too well what being alone is like. It's not the best feeling in the world."

Maya's mother shook her head in disbelief, hair loosening from its bound state. "The one I hurt most is the one who comes to help. It's always been said do unto others as you would have them do unto you." She shook her head vigorously. "There is no way I'd expect you to help me, Maya. It would be too much."

Maya clasped her mother's hands. "You don't have to ask me to do this. I want to. By helping you, I'm helping myself. I'm not the only victim my father had. We're both in need of forgiving ourselves. We've been bound for so long, we're used to living with things. It would be nice to know what being free is like.."

She smoothed her mother's hair back. "We need to release the hurt, Mama. We can do that. It's harder to release it than it is to live with it. But we can do this, Mama. We're strong like that. If we survived what he and others did to us, we can handle so much more — if you're willing to try."

Her mother nodded, trembling slightly. "Yes, Maya. I think I can do that."

Maya put her hands on the face of the woman she had feared for so long. Her mother's tears streamed down her face. Maya knelt in front of her and looked into her eyes. Their gaze stayed locked for what seemed an eternity.

Finally her mother smiled and nodded. "I see you, Maya. I really see you now. You are nothing like him. And nothing like me. You have a compassion that neither one of us had. You are so beautiful. I don't deserve to say that I'm your mother."

Maya touched her face, blinking to clear her vision. "Now I know where I get my strength." Maya embraced her mother once again, then laid her head on her mother's lap, and closed her eyes. Tears streamed steadily onto her mother's clothes.

Her mother stroked her soft hair lightly, as she looked down at her baby girl. For the first time, Maya's mother reached out a hand to Maya — in love and compassion.

ction:

RELEASING/FORGIVENESS: On New Year's Eve, members of my church and their families do a physical, but symbolic act of cleansing in a service. We make a list of things we don't want in our lives any longer and put them on the altar. It's a time for us to clean out, get rid of our emotional baggage, get rid of the resentment allows us to get rid of the fear.

And fear comes in all kinds of ways. It has a million different costumes, but when it comes we have to say, "The Lord, The Creator, has not given me a spirit of fear, but the power of love, and a sound mind."

That is what God has given each one of us. And when we begin to use that power, fear begins to dissipate. Fear can be resentment and anger. Fear is being judgmental and critical. Fear is looking at the lack and limitation man has put in our path, but God has not.

As we begin to stay in the presence of God, we're laying a foundation so no matter what comes we can say, "My God told me I could overcome this. I don't know how it's going to work out. I don't know what will happen but I know God's going to do it because that's his commitment to me."

As we begin to stay in that consciousness, we become new and improved, rejuvenated and power-packed because that's what it's all about. We welcome the challenges that move us onto a new path. And that path where God is, where the Christ Consciousness is, becomes so embedded in us that no matter what man says, we know what God has said is true.

Every day we should cleanse our mind and release unwanted thoughts, feelings, attitudes, and habits from our consciousness. Release it and let go. Let go and let God take care of it. As we begin to release and let go, our hearts and minds are filled with Divine Love, Divine Healing, and Divine Health because God is there.

As a songwriter once wrote: "What the world needs now, is love, sweet love. It's the only thing that there's just too little of."

*A**ffirmation:* "The love of God lives in me and I live in the love of God. I love and approve of myself and bring loving situations, people, and events into my environment — right now. And so it is."

*ersonal recipe*

In most cases survivors of domestic violence and/or sexual assault are laden with so much guilt, that one of the things they want to start off with is loving and appreciating who they are as a gift from God. Starting with a simple affirmation such as: I love and approve of myself unconditionally, saying it as many times as possible throughout the day, can work wonders.

TRUDY

CHALLENGE: FINDING HER SPIRITUAL PATH

AGE: **34**

STATUS: **SINGLE MOTHER**

OCCUPATION: **COMPUTER PROGRAMMER**

SPIRITUAL BACKGROUND: **BAPTIST/METHODIST/APOSTOLIC/**
HEBREW ISRAELITE/ISLAM/AUSAR-AUSET/SCIENCE OF MIND

After several painful episodes in my life, I searched for answers. In so doing, I've experienced several belief systems, trying to find my spiritual path.

After being molested by my father and an uncle, I believed this world held no true beauty; only a false image of what it's suppose to be. I started searching for answers. I didn't join any of the temples or churches I attended during my search. This was purely a search for knowledge and understanding. I wanted to know something about every religion that appealed to me. I wanted to understand why my innocence had been taken from me and why ugly things kept happening to me.

One thing I found is that I didn't want to hear about a God of vengeance and punishment, fire, and brimstone; a God whose sole purpose was to catch us and punish us if we did something wrong. If that was what God was like, then I didn't want to believe in God.

I wanted religion, but not the structured forms in which I grew up. At one point I visited the mosque and exlored the Nation of Islam for a while. As I listened to its teachings, I gave up pork and even became a vegetarian for a short period of time. (That is, until I passed a little fast-food place near my house, and went through chicken withdrawal. I had a six-piece special with mild barbecue sauce and didn't feel a pinch of guilt — until I paid for it a little later.)

But all dietary requirements aside, when I thought about a structured religion, I wanted to have a better spiritual base. I knew one thing: I didn't want to believe in God because I was scared into believing. I wanted to love God because it was in my nature to do so.

I now believe in a Creator or God that represents peace, beauty, love, prosperity, and abundance. I believe that everyone and everything has its place in creation. I don't allow any religion to separate me from this belief. I appreciate all of them. I believe there is an element of truth in every religion and the one that is right for each of us is something only our inner spirit can help us find. However, not everyone can see or appreciate that fact.

In my search, I knew I didn't want to practice one given religion, but if I did, it would have to be one that had a tolerance for other religions — and not too many of them do that. One would say, if you don't do a, b, and c then you're going to hell. Or if you don't do a combination of c, b, and z, you're going there, too. Or if you even entertain or listen to the concepts of a belief system other than theirs, you're headed straight for the fire.

I'm not saying that all religions should accept or embrace the differences in other doctrines, but I don't believe that followers of any one religion are heaven-bound and everyone else is headed down a path leading straight to hell. If the focus was on their own truth, and individuals truly understand their chosen way, there would be little talk about religions in a way that makes others seem inferior. When I listen to people who believe that way, it's a real turn-off. Finding a place to worship took almost fourteen years.

I grew up Baptist, switched to Methodist, then to Apostolic. When I didn't receive the "gift of tongues" in the Apostolic's tarry room, as they said was necessary, I remained without a religion. Later, I studied with the Hebrew Israelites where I gained an appreciation for my color and the struggle.

When I reached Metaphysics and Science of Mind, that's where I felt the most comfortable. I learned that spirituality is deeper than just religion or what people look like on the outside. The focus was on spirituality and not a set way of doing things. There were positive affirmations and the belief that there was nothing in the Universe which could not be changed — even for me. I still read materials and study guides from all religions, because encouraging words can be found anywhere we look for them. But I don't feel bound, I feel enlightened and I believe that's what the Creator intended.

When I pray now, I begin my prayers by saying "to Mother-Father God," because the Creator has been both for me. My real mother and father were not good representations of the Creator's love, wisdom, and understanding.

I still look for the beauty in life that represents the Creator even with all that happened. At the times when my life was most painful, I didn't give up on the Creator. And I truly believe the Creator didn't give up on me. I never believed that. I've been given a small sampling of what the Creator is like with my new spiritual family and positive friendships. I thank my Mother-Father God daily for what has been given me and ask the Creator to bless those I care about.

Instead of accepting what most were accustomed to, I searched and searched for a place where I could worship and be healed. Prayer, Praise, and Faith has been just that type of place. Sesvalah has been a blessing to me and so have the members who have embraced me like a long lost child. Because truly there have been times in my life that I was lost, confused and in pain.

With counseling and an acceptance that spirituality doesn't necessarily mean being part of an organized or structured religion, my emotional and physical pains have subsided. I am filled with joy and a sense of peace which only comes with knowing that I am part of a larger universe of people and we each have our own set of challenges to overcome and our own path.

My challenges are dealt with on a daily basis, because healing is perpetual. Whereas before sadness, depression, and self-loathing were a big part of my existence, they have been replaced with peace, happiness, and self-love — things I never believed would enter so easily into my heart and mind.

I thank the Creator for Sesvalah. I thank the Creator for the members of my worship center because they have been teachers and blessings for me in human form.

Personal recipe _____

Pull out your personal journal or the Speak it into Existence journal. Take a moment to jot down information that came to mind as you read this chapter. Then write down your own formula for speaking it into existence. It can be an affirmation, Bible verse, mantra, etc., but it should be something that you'll use everyday until you see your desire come into existence.

LISSA

CHALLENGE: **WANTS TO BE A CEO OF HER OWN PUBLISHING COMPANY**

AGE: **34**

STATUS: **SINGLE MOTHER**

OCCUPATION: **AUTHOR, BUSINESS WOMAN**

SPIRITUAL BACKGROUND: **B'HAI**

One day, after a grueling day at work, made even more so by the fact I'd been up most of the night writing and planning, my boss called me into his office when he saw me taking the second set of pain pills that day. "You're working too hard. I know you're trying to get out of here." (It was no secret that I wanted leave my job as a legal secretary). "I know you want to do something different with your life and start your own business."

I glanced at the file cabinet behind him, filled with information on his IRAs, stocks, bonds, and mutual funds. The man was loaded. I pointed and said, "I don't have any one of those, so I have to come up with something else. There's no guarantee that Social Security will be solvent when I retire. Pensions are being sucked dry by crooked employers these days, leaving people who have paid into them for years holding an empty bag."

David blinked twice and didn't say a word.

I took a long, slow breath before saying, "If something happened to me right now, my son has only my life insurance policy to live on. And that's not enough. He's going to college and I don't want him to start his life in debt like I did. Someone in our family has to improve where we stand. That person is me. Jeremy shouldn't know what debt is. His children shouldn't know either.

"My mother worked for the state until she was sixty-three and retired. She died two years later without getting a chance to enjoy her time off, or to enjoy herself while her body could keep up. That's not going to happen to me."

David listened attentively.

"If something happens and I need to have a transplant, I don't have the money to buy a kidney." I smiled. "Hell, if I need to kill somebody to get that kidney, I don't have the money to pay an assassin." (Forgive me, people, I have a wicked sense of humor).

David laughed, which is exactly what I wanted. (For the purposes of this book, and in the words of *my* lawyer, I am **not** endorsing the unlawful act of soliciting murder).

"But you have health insurance."

"Yes, but I have an HMO and you know some things aren't covered."

With that he reached into his drawer, took out his checkbook, scribbled something, and passed me a check. "Will this help with your new business?"

I almost broke down in tears in the man's office!

This was the start of something good. With those funds I started a publishing house and printed the first novel, *The Things I Could Tell You!*, by a teenage author (J. L. Woodson) In the following pages, I'll recount the story the same way it was published in *How to Win the Publishing Game* to encourage others to follow their dreams:

Being a legal secretary was not the way Lissa wanted to spend the rest of her life. She loved writing and had penned six novels in two years. Not only did she want to write, she wanted to publish others who had good stories to tell, but couldn't seem to find much success with major publishing houses. Her son was almost finished with his novel, and Lissa figured she'd take two months to put together the initial money to print it and the promotional material. That was enough time to save the money out of her paychecks, but leave enough money to take care of her son and pay the bills.

However, things were put in fast-forward when Maureen Cronin of Borders Books and Café called to place an order for J. L.'s novel, which Lissa had mentioned to them a few weeks before when she had come in to purchase something.

Maureen had met J. L. and wanted to have his books released first in their store. They needed the novel in two weeks, when the store was expecting a group of high school students. Borders wanted J.L. to talk with the group about writing and encourage other students to become writers.

Lissa started to say, "impossible," then shut her mouth, said a quick prayer, and told the manager, "It can happen."

Well, problem one — printers take four weeks to finish a book. She had less than two. Trevy McDonald, a fellow author and friend, had recently given her information about a digital printing company that had turned her book around pretty fast. Lissa had already called them for a quote and had it on file. As soon as she hung up with Borders, Lissa called Denny, her sales person. "Remember that job we spoke about three days ago?"

"Yes."

"Well, you can have the job."

"Great."

She swallowed hard. "If you can have it finished and delivered to me for a book signing on January 24."

Silence.

"Denny?"

"I don't think we can do that. We're fast but not *that* fast."

"Could you check?"

"I'll call you right back."

Lissa said another quick prayer. When the phone rang five minutes later, she snatched it up on the first ring.

Denny said, "We can do it, but only if we get the files from you by Monday."

Lissa sighed. Monday was three days away. "I'll get on it."

Problem one solved. Now, on to the next problem. The book wasn't even finished! People were still reading it to check for last minute errors. Problem three — no matter how much Lissa wanted to help him, J.L. would have to be the one to input those changes — usually a slow process for him. Problem four, she had just given the computer to Devon, one of the technicians at her job. He was supposed to have the computer back to her Monday. Her son wouldn't have any way to work on the manuscript even if he did have the pages in front of him.

Lissa picked up the phone and dialed. "Devon, I have an emergency. I know you said the computer would be ready on Monday, but I just got a call and my son needs to finish the book this weekend.

Devon hesitated before saying. "I don't know."

"Devon, please. If we miss this coming out of the gate—."

"All right, come on down. I'll do it after I get off work."

"Thanks."

Next, Lissa called one of her bosses who she knew would be working late. "Hillary, I know you're still working on the novel, but I just got a call and now we have to finish it and turn it over to the printer by Monday. So I'll just have J.L. work on what you have."

"I left the manuscript at home."

Lissa's heart did an underside flip. Her boss had carried that manuscript back and forth every day to work on catching errors. And on *this* day she chose to leave it at home!

"Okay, I'll need to come to your house tonight and pick it up if that's all right with you."

"Sure, I'll give you the directions."

"I still have to come into the office to pick up my computer and then I'll come to your place after that."

Not having a car, Lissa took the train to work. Devon had the hard drive sitting on her desk. As soon as she picked it up to put it on the cart, the phone rang.

It was J.L. and he was in a panic. "Mom, Maureen called. Borders want 250 books. Don't they realize we don't have a book yet? What are we gonna do?"

Lissa laughed. He sounded just as she had when she first received the call. Maureen had left a message on her son's voicemail as well. "Don't worry, I have the computer and I'm on my way to Hillary's to get her changes. You'll have to finish them up tonight. Are you up for it?"

"You bet!"

"Good, because it has to be finished and on its way to the printer by Monday."

"What about Mr. Bretz's changes?"

"We haven't heard from your old teacher and I don't think he'll get it back to us in time for this round."

"Well, I'm glad Susan had a chance to look at it twice."

Susan Mary Malone was his editor and she had helped Jeremy develop an English assignment and entries from his lifetime journal into a full-fledged novel. "I'll see you when I get home."

Lissa scooped the computer off her desk and used a cab voucher to get to Hillary's home. The voucher, a company courtesy, would allow the money for the cab fare to come out of her paycheck a month later. Lissa arrived at Hillary's home, picked up the manuscript, then the cab took her home.

She passed the manuscript to J. L. and he went to work. She got on the phone with the cover designer and worked out the final details. He would have it on Tuesday, which was good timing. The printer was more interested in having the text (the insides of the book), since that took the longest to setup in their digital system.

J.L. stayed up until 3:30 a.m., pounding away on Hillary's changes. He came into Lissa's room, eyes bloodshot red. "Mom, I can't do anymore tonight. I still want to go to class tomorrow."

J.L. was in a Saturday entrepreneurial class with the Chicago Urban League; it taught him how to manage money, stocks and bonds, which he enjoyed. "Okay, print out what you've done and I'll double-check Hillary's suggestion against what you actually typed in."

"Okay. Night, Mom."

Lissa knew J. L. would finish on time. Now, the next problem: money. She didn't get paid for another five days, but she would have to send half of the money when she submitted the print job. She didn't have it. Lissa had already called Sesvalah, her minister, and said, "Hey, some very good things are happening, but at the worst possible time."

Sesvalah listened to Lissa's story. "It's the *best* possible situation. The Creator will manifest in ways you can't see right now. Do the work, but leave the details to the Creator." With that, Lissa forged ahead as if she already had the money to do everything she needed.

Saturday, while Jeremy was at class, Lissa received a call from Dr. House, a fellow church member. "Hey, I hear there's some wonderful things going on with Macro Publishing Group. How can I help?"

Only Sesvalah could have mentioned that to Dr. House because she was the only one, except those involved with the book, Lissa had talked to since Borders placed the order. She explained what was going on and then Dr. House said, "I'll bring a check with me tomorrow. How much do you need?"

Lissa nearly fainted! Instead, she thanked the Creator for circulating prosperity through the universe and down to her little corner of the world.

Based on earlier suggestions from her son, Lissa included poetry and affirmations from his favorite people in every chapter. Some were also authors who would eventually be published under her company, and others were people who had helped Lissa and her son all their lives. While Jeremy was in class she had worked in the affirmations and poems that he circled and finished laying out the book. Jeremy finished the novel that night after class.

The next day she took the galleys (a prepress version of the book) of her son's novel with her to church, and she testified to the completion of the book and what had been requested by Borders. She also told of the Creator sending her the help she needed. After service, a few of the members sat around looking the book over, making suggestions, and giving insight to things that Lissa, in a total rush, had missed. The first print run would be small, but then she would have Christine Meister, a second editor, look it over again before they went to press for the second run.

The book went to the printers without a hitch. The cover was done and sent two days later.

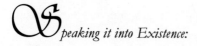

peaking it into Existence:

The Creator has never stopped the commitment to us. Because we've made a commitment to the Creator, we must listen to that still, small voice. As we do, we begin to see more of the Creator manifesting wonderful things in our lives. Our eyes become open so we can see the goodness of the Creator in everything that happens.

We just have to begin to know that there is one true source and that source is the Creator. Before this, Lissa would never have believed that her boss would have helped fund her dreams, especially since he knew that when she was successful, she would be leaving and he would have to find another secretary.

As we begin to look to the Creator for whatever it is, then people, places, and opportunities become evident everywhere.

LISSA PART II

CHALLENGE: LACK OF MONEY SUBSTANCE

With the books off to the printer, Lissa thought she could breathe, but then she received a call from her son's principal, Ms. Hawkins. "We want to be the first ones to get a copy of Jeremy's novel. We will need four hundred copies of the book."

The cover designer had been paid, the editor had been paid, invoices for the bookmarks, posters, business cards, and other promotional material had been paid, and her personal bills had been paid. Lissa didn't have the money to print more books.

Ms. Hawkins asked, "How much will it be?"

Lissa gave her the amount and Ms. Hawkins said, "I'll cut a check and we'll pick up our copies at Borders."

This was on Sunday. Monday was a school holiday so Lissa expected to pick up the check on Tuesday and send it off to the printer. Lissa increased the order.

Unfortunately, when Lissa went to pick up the check on Tuesday, Ms. Hawkins had been called out of town on an emergency. There was no way that Lissa could get the money to the printer in time. If she didn't get the money to them, they wouldn't ship *any* of her books. This was her first job with the company and she had not established credit with them. Lissa tried to keep her anxiety at bay. She kept saying, "The Lord is My Shepherd and I shall not want," as her affirmation.

The next day one of the authors, whose novels Lissa had been helping to complete, called. "Come over and see what I've been working on."

Lissa sighed, and thought, "I really have to focus on getting the money for Jeremy's novel." But she followed her inner voice and went to the woman's office.

Completely unaware of Lissa's financial predicament, Ms. Mason gave her acheck that was only $200 short of what she needed for the printing company.

When Lissa arrived at her home, she found a $200 check from Sesvalah in her mailbox!

Everything was set and the books would be delivered two days before the signing. People had been calling and placing more orders. Lissa wasn't going to increase the order again. Every one else would have to wait for the next print run.

Lissa and J.L. pulled up in front of Borders fifteen minutes before they were due for the signing. A group of two hundred students from Triumphant Charter School were there. The line snaked around the corner and Borders had to open a half hour early to accommodate the large crowd. Another group of one hundred fifty students and teachers from Chavez School arrived an hour later.

Earlier, Maureen called and told Lissa that the students J. L. had been invited to speak to wouldn't have the money to purchase the novels. The manager was wrong. That second group pooled their money and bought as many as they could afford.

Just as J.L. was about to take a break, another group of students from Mighty God Christian Academy showed up. He watched them pour out of the vans. "Well, there goes my break." Then, just as he finally took a bite out of a sandwich, another group of students from his school, Olive-Harvey Middle College showed up two hundred strong. By the time 1 p.m. rolled around, J. L. had almost sold out of books. But people continued to come to the table and request a copy. The number dwindled down to a mere thirteen books by 1:30. From that point on, Borders had to take pre-orders for the next print-run. Even without books left for them to buy, people still wanted to meet J. L. and asked him to sign posters and bookmarks. Overall, more than 700 people showed up for J. L.'s first signing, including a talk show host with a camera crew.

But that wasn't the end. As things had started to come together to get J. L.'s book printed in time to meet the deadlines, Lissa thought that she and J. L. needed to somehow thank and show appreciation to all the people who had supported them. Those people who reached into their own pockets to help meet the costs, and who had showed faith in the project in so many ways.

Lissa planned a party for them the night of the book release at Don Pablos Mexican Kitchen. She sure didn't have the money to pay for it, but she just knew (all the signs were there) that the book signing would be successful enough to provide the money for the party. And it was. Not only that, but the restaurant did more than just accommodate all the people on the guest list — they supplied more food than Lissa had ordered. People were so full they were almost glued to their chairs!

Lissa was so excited she didn't go to sleep until almost three hours after she and J.L. got home. She thanked the Creator for allowing the earth "angels" and her personal angels to facilitate such a successful event. She had been ready to say it was "impossible." But the situations and events leading up to the sold-out book signing showed her that nothing was impossible for them who believe.

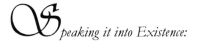

Speaking it into Existence:

As in the case of the other accounts in this book, Lissa also paid attention to the still, small voice that guided her to saying and doing just the right thing at the right time, eventually leading to the perfect results. Everyone — Maureen, David, Dr. House, Devon, Hillary, and all the other people she encountered in her path to her goals — were beneficial in helping her achieve that goal. Lissa's story is especially close to my heart because her company —Macro Publishing Group — published the book you are reading. The next few pages complete her story and show, once again, that the Creator will supply our needs in a most unusual way.

LISSA (PART III)

Now on to the next challenge. Borders called less than three days after the book release asking for J.L. to attend four new book signing events. Then the Illinois Bureau of Unemployment Insurance called requesting him to come and speak and bring two hundred books. Then Tracy Fletcher of Merry Green Promotions Group asked for him to be on a panel of authors for V103s Expo for Today's Woman — an event which more than 100,000 people attend each year. All of these requests were for major events! Unfortunately, Lissa was back to square one — Borders would take at least sixty days to process her check for the sale of the books from J.L.'s first signing.

She would need to have several thousand books printed within the next three weeks. It was a tight schedule and she would have to go with an offset (web) printer, not the digital one she used for the first printing. The difference would be in paying $3.36 per book versus $1.54 per book. With all the requests from television and radio stations for copies of his books and media kits, she needed the books as fast as she could get them. With two entire paychecks she would still be a few hundred dollars short — again.

Lissa sat down to do her budget. "I don't think I'll see a paycheck for myself until two months from now." Then she corrected her statement by saying, "Cancel that thought. The Creator will open doors for me and make a way."

She had the first half of the money when she turned in the files to the printer. But when she read the small print in the contract, she found some requirements that she wasn't sure how to complete. The pictures and advertisement she put in the back of the novel required some special treatment to turn them from color to black and white and they preferred a particular format if the pictures were placed inside the document. She didn't have a clue how to do this but it would cost her extra if the company did it for her.

Then the printer sent her an e-mail stating that they expected to have the files in their office the next day and they wanted them in their down state office and not the Chicago office. Her first thought was to allow J.L. to make the last of his changes, then she would work on creating the new pages and messenger the files the next morning. Sending a messenger was not an option.

Her editor, Christine, had been working on the novel all week and had been giving the changes to J.L. as she finished. They still had sixty pages to go. Plus Lissa had promised to give three other authors the opportunity to have information about their novels printed in the back of the novel. She had to create their pages, correct the color and format of all the pictures, and wait for J.L. to finish Christine's changes.

All of this had to be done in *two hours* and then she'd have to get back downtown to have the package in the Federal Express office before 9 p.m. Since she got off work at 5 and didn't get home until 5:45, Lissa thought she wouldn't make the deadline; she'd have to go with the digital printer again.

She nearly cried as she talked with the sales rep, who then offered to drive the files to the downstate office if she sent it by messenger to his home by 10:30 p.m. This opened up a little more time, but she desperately wanted to make the Federal Express deadline — because it was cheaper.

At 4:47 p.m. while still at work, David called her into his office and asked her what was wrong. Lissa, who had kept her challenges to herself, gave him a little of what was going on. "I didn't realize that starting my own company entailed so much. I had a comfortable plan that went out of the window as soon as the first call came in from Borders. I've been on the hot seat ever since."

David listened and gave her a few words of comfort before adding, "Get going and get that boy's book done. You can handle it." In order to make the deadline, she would have to finish by 8 p.m. Finally, after she went through her panic mode (her normal reaction to challenges), she prayed, talked with David, and settled down — she went home and tried to do everything. Her son sat in the room with her to keep encouraging her, then he hit her with a bomb: "My class goes to Hawaii next week."

Lissa stopped typing. "Why didn't you remind me?"

"Because I'm not going."

"I can print a lot fewer books and you can go on your trip. You shouldn't miss being with your class because of my dreams of starting a company and publishing good books."

Her son sat up on his bed and looked her square in the eye. "Mom, in a minute, I'll be able to take everyone I know to Hawaii."

Lissa nearly cried. Her son had more faith than she did at times.

She finished at 8:01 p.m. J.L. had already called a cab. She waited until 8:11, when the document was almost finished printing to call back a second time. "The cab is on its way, ma'am." 8:20 and still no cab. The cab didn't hear the first call. It's on its way." Finally, the cab showed at 8:29! It would take at least thirty minutes driving the speed limit just to get downtown and another five minutes to get to Federal Express.

J. L. said, "Mom, we'll make it."

If they hit any construction traffic — they wouldn't make it. If the car broke down — they wouldn't make it. If they drove the speed limit — they wouldn't. Luckily, the driver didn't know what a speed limit was. He punched it to eighty and when they hit traffic, he swerved off the expressway to a side street until traffic eased up, then slipped back on the expressway.

They pulled up in front of Federal Express at 8:55 and Jeremy ran up the street waving the envelope and label and rushed into the office at 8:58. They made it!

But that was only the beginning. The printer called two days later to tell her, "Your cover is too large for this job. It might have been perfect for the digital job, but we use a thinner paper. The edges will be cut off along with the author's name."

This was a major problem. She thought one cover fit all. Her cover designer was on a plane to Nigeria and she had no way of contacting him. And if she couldn't get the cover back to the printer, they would not be able to keep her printing schedule. Orders continued to stream in every day.

As she sat in her office, performing the duties of her nine-to-five, Lissa came up with an inspired idea. She called the company who had printed her son's promotional posters, bookmarks, and business cards. They said they would be able to convert the cover. She called the digital printer and they sent her the files to give to the media company. The media company fixed the file and sent it to the printer. It was only a day later. Lissa breathed a sigh of relief.

Then the printer called again. "The cover is spread too far. When we print the cover, some of the words will still be cut off."

Lissa slumped in her chair. "I can have the media company correct it."

"There's no time. They obviously aren't as knowledgeable about book-cover specifications and it's going to cost another $89 to reconstruct it from the Internet again."

Lissa had already paid an additional $80 when they first tried to correct the cover — all for nothing.

"Okay, I'll just go digital."

"I'm sorry things didn't work out."

"Yeah, me too."

Lissa put her head down on the desk for a few moments and prayed. Then she called the digital printer and requested a quote for half the number of books she had planned to print with the offset company — far fewer than she needed. Her son had given up his class trip for nothing!

Lissa went about her day and was startled when a call came in from the offset printer. "I think I've found a way to handle this."

"Oh?" Lissa was all ears.

"We have a copy of the book that was done with the digital printer. One of our second-shift guys found some of that paper the digital printer used here in-house. We don't normally use it and it will cost a lot more."

"Really?"

"Yes, it's a wider sheet for the press, but we'll be able to use the cover you sent us and it won't require any changes."

Lissa would have to find the money from somewhere. "Run the job. I'll work it out."

"And we'll be able to finish the books on schedule."

"Thanks."

Lissa had just laid her head on her desk when one of the people from accounting stopped by to say hi. Judy took one look at Lissa and escorted her to an empty conference room where Lissa could vent and get herself together. The job had cost $400 more than she had been prepared for, plus she still had to pay the balance. Her next paycheck wouldn't cover it as she had planned, but she said another prayer.

When she got back to her desk, the printer had sent an e-mail with the balance. Lissa called accounting to find out exactly what her paycheck would be. The news wasn't good. She was not going to make it. *After this one, maybe I should rethink this publishing thing and just stick to writing and getting an agent. This is major challenge after challenge.*

Judy stopped by to wish Lissa a happy birthday. Lissa had totally forgotten it *was* her birthday. Judy, who had read Jeremy's manuscript and made changes for both printings, whispered in Lissa's ear, "I believe in what you're doing, and I believe in what you're doing for your son."

Judy walked away. Lissa looked down at her desk a few minutes later to pull out her budget and $320 in twenties stared back. Judy had put it there! Lissa's heart soared as she called Judy to thank her, but voicemail kicked in. She went up to accounting but Judy wasn't there. She'd have to thank her another time.

An hour later, one of the authors who had become more like a mother to Lissa, called and asked if she would stop by that evening to get the rest of the changes for an upcoming book. While they worked on the manuscript, the woman slipped Lissa a tiny envelope with a card. Lissa opened it and four thin, crisp, hundred dollar bills fell onto her lap. Lissa hugged the woman and held back tears. The woman said, "Happy birthday, baby."

It truly was.

And it became an even better birthday when Dr. House said, "Hey, I'm in on this printing, too. Come and pick up a check on Friday." Dr. House would get her return for the first printing, and the second one, out of the check from Borders which would come any day. So this was just another investment and Lissa would still come out ahead. The Borders check would enable Lissa to pay back all the women and still have a stream of income coming in from the $2,000 she would have on tap. The pre-orders were still flooding in.

Lissa took out money from her checking account, combined it with the cash from Dr. House, and put it in a cashier's check, sealed it into a Federal Express envelope and thanked the Creator for earthly and spiritual assistance.

The books arrived on schedule and the orders still kept coming in. A few days later, Lissa turned to Jeremy on their way home from a successful book signing. "I think Hawaii would be nice in a couple of months."

Jeremy smiled. "No doubt about it."

Note from Lissa: That wasn't fiction. It's told it exactly how it happened. Unlike large houses, who at one time were small houses, my cash flow came the hard way. I work a 9-to-5 job as a legal secretary. There wasn't any cash available to me when I decided to publish the first novel. I used what I had, but people sometimes make the mistake of thinking help only comes from sources they create (like my paycheck). My goal was to send out sponsor packages and get money in that manner. After the first call from Maureen, there wasn't any time for that.

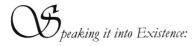 *peaking it into Existence:*

The Creator, in the Divine Plan, brings circumstances that not only test our faith and desire — but confirm that we are working in Divine Order. I had several tests throughout that thirteen-day process — some were pop-up quizzes — others were final exams. We already have the ultimate source of prosperity as it has been promised to each one of us. All we have to do is put things in motion and everything will come in divine time.

Most business people would say that I shouldn't have started my company until I lined up everything and a substantial cash flow. That would have taken months, possibly years. My story proves that having a strong, but positive desire, if not the funds, will put people in our path to help and encourage us. What it takes is for us to have purpose, have faith, and then get off your butt and do the work.

ction:

Immediately begin to speak the words to counteract the doubt and fear: "My God shall supply my needs. There is no lack in God."

Put forth some form of action — to keep your faith working on your behalf. Buy envelopes to mail out invitations if you want to have a party (at little or no cost), pack your suitcase for a vacation — whether you know how, when or where.

I wanted to go to California to visit my Godparents but at the time I had no money. I decided would go any way, called my Godparents, told them I was coming with no knowledge of how. I chose what I wanted to wear, packed my suitcase, and thanked God everyday for my wonderful vacation in California right now. Money just came from everywhere — unexpected sources. Within days my vacation was paid for in full.

ffirmation:

In the Bible we are told: Beloved, I wish abundance above all things that thou mayest prosper and be in health, even as thy soul prospereth.

We must remember that the Creator wants us to prosper and no good thing will be withheld. We must claim our victory through the creative force within us. "Thank you Lord that all my bills are paid and my life is in Divine Order."

Each one of us has a path that the Creator has put out there for us. They may not all be the same. Our path may be to give a word of encouragement to every person that comes in our lives, or to send out Divine Love and Healing to make someone feel better. That's what it means to be an ambassador. That's what God is about, helping people have hope. Letting them know that there's something else they can see besides the darkness. You might just have a smile for someone. Because sometimes that's all a person needs — someone to smile at them or to give them an uplifting word — to help them to go a little further.

There are so many people who are sad, who are depressed, who are down and have no hope. Being an ambassador means coming out of who you are. It means you can't stay in depression or sadness yourself and be so overwhelmed with what you think is real. That means that as we are transformed, we see past the illusion. We don't see the bills, we see that God has already taken care of them. And we believe that there's abundance and a never-ending supply.

God said that there's always a ram in the bush, just like he left for Abraham who had prepared to sacrifice his own son. He already has a ram in the bush for each one of us as we continue to be transformed by the renewal of our minds.

On another note, one of the authors whose novel was set to be published later that year, sent J.L. and Lissa on a week-long trip to Hawaii, just two months after the release of J.L.'s second printing. Recently both Lissa and J.L. were given seperate three book deals with a major publishing house

Truly we should always thank the Creator that we are open and receptive and know that every seeming challenge is already taken care of. The Creator is the only source of our income and will meet us at our point of need — in ways we couldn't begin to imagine.

Personal recipe

Pull out your personal journal or the Speak it into Existence journal. Take a moment to jot down information that came to mind as you read this chapter. Then write down your own formula for speaking it into existence. It can be an affirmation, Bible verse, mantra, etc., but it should be something that you'll use everyday until you see your desire come into existence.

Speaking it into Existence:

How do we do this? The holy book states that faith is the substance of things hoped for and the evidence of things unseen. It also states that there is life and death in the tongue and that we should hold on to our confession of faith.

"Faith" or "belief" is the actual building block of desire. It creates the dream, the vision or the goal. It is the evidence of the object of our desire — which means that even though we can't see it, feel it, or hear it in the natural third-dimensional world — it still is and we must continue to claim it as such. Remembering that if we look around, everything we see, feel, hear, taste or touch — the table, the pages of this book, the clothes we wear, the cars we drive, etc., were once a dream or a vision or desire in someone's heart.

The Creator has given us the power to create with our own mouth, speaking words of confession can create the life that we desire or one that we do not want. We must be diligent in speaking only those things we want to see. We can't confess prosperity in one breath and then state we're poor or broke in another. The tongue and thoughts must be on one accord.

Let's say that we desire to go to college. Start by spending a little private time with the Creator — listening to the still, small voice of direction and wisdom that is within each one of us. Then pray, affirm, or state our intention.

For example: *Dear Mother-Father God, Creator of all that is or ever will be, I desire to attend the perfect college for me with all the support I need, harmonious relationships, money to pay all expenses, a creative-learning environmental, the perfect housing situation, professors and instructions that are the perfect teachers for me to grow, etc. Thank you Lord that this is so."*

After the prayer, start moving forward toward your goals, watching for signs (remember Faith without works is dead). Investigate the different colleges all the while confessing through the spoken word that you are "attending the perfect college." Thank you Lord that I have been accepted into the perfect college, all expenses paid. Hold onto your confession of faith.

Things will begin to fall in place. Someone will be talking about a college, or we will see an advertisement and be on our way. We must remember that our words must be consistent with our desires. When those doubts come — and they will — quickly confess your faith; quickly state your desire in the now, quickly repeat any affirmation that you have developed to stay focus on your goal.

*ffirmation:*

Just as God gave Solomon all wisdom, knowledge, and understanding, I am filled with the spirit of God who knows all and I am guided and directed to my perfect [____fill in____].

Perfect love casts out all fear. The perfect love of God lives in me now and forever.

God has not given me a spirit of fear but of power, love and sound mind, I stand knowing that all is well in my mind, body, and life.

The perfect love of God lives in my heart and I attract perfect love to me right now. I release resentment and all it affects in my life. I release it in perfect harmony right now. I open myself to the perfect flow of the Universe.

Remember always — the power of the spoken word directs the flow of your life. Whichever thought has the most power is the thought that brings results.

I would like to leave you with these thoughts:

We are over-comers, and as we stay in the essence of who God is, nothing can defeat us. Even though it may look difficult, we have to say, "There is no defeat in God. I'm already an achiever and an over-comer and winner. There's no defeat where God is." And so as we say these words to whatever situation, any seeming challenge dissipates into the nothing that is. And we continue to see the transformation of God in our lives. "Be ye transformed by the renewing of your mind." It also means that we continue to treat each other with love.

We have to treat each other with compassion. And not only each other, but treat ourselves with love and compassion. Because many times we criticize ourselves, we find fault by saying: I should have done this, I should look this way, I should say that. I should be this way, or that way.

Instead of judging yourself, love yourself. Look at yourself and love every pound of you. Love every inch of you. Love yourself from the top of your head to the soles of your feet. And just watch all those things that need to be changed or transformed because you begin to love who you are.

Remember, your body is the temple of the Living God. How could you not love where God resides? The Creator wants us to be transformed by the principle of love and if we do everything in love, then we just continue to transform our lives.

As we walk around, abundance comes from everywhere because we become the magnet of love.

Jesus didn't have any money, but he was taken care of in the fashion of kings because people took care of him. Help came to him wherever he traveled. He knew the principle of abundance and that's what Jesus came to teach us — how we, in these human bodies, could do the things he had done.

It's just like a big brother, who having learned or mastered something new, would show his little sister or brother, "Hey, come check this out. Look what I can do." After demonstrating this new ability, the younger sibling would try it too. And he/she would keep trying until they mastered it. Because his/her brother had done it, he/she didn't think it was impossible.

Jesus, our elder brother, showed us the way Faith and works brought about miracles. He took the five loaves of bread and two fish, and somehow made them multiply until they took care of the people's needs. As we become transformed by that principle of love, we have the ability to take that same five loaves of bread and two fish in our lives (in whatever form they may come) and transform them into whatever we need today.

Don't allow outside stuff to come in and take us off the target. Don't allow bill collectors to make us fearful of answering the phone or opening a letter. We're not going to allow someone else to make us fearful of going to a job, or coming to our own homes. We know that God is, and because God is, there is no fear. We know that we are given a spirit that is filled with power, love and a sound mind — not of fear. And that's how we're being transformed so as we walk, doors just begin to open for us.

Every Red Sea (challenge) spreads itself for us. And as we step into the lake, it moves out of the way, just like when Aaron, of the Old Testament, carried the ark. He stepped in the water and it just moved out of the way. It should be the same way with us. The Bible and many other spiritual books have several examples of the Creator manifesting in many ways.

This is a time of renewal, this is a time of foundation building. This is a time of overcoming. This is a time when the spirit of God is touching everything in and around us. We have to focus on love, just love — even when other things look like they need our attention. Focus on the principle of love. Everything we do should be in the consciousness of love, speaking in love, teaching in love, and touching in love. If we think God has given us miracles thus far, once we begin to do this, things in our lives will make a three hundred-and-sixty degree turn for the better.

What do we think God is? God created the heaven and the earth and right now that heaven and earth can be created where we are. What is it that we want to create? What is it that we want to see in our life? What is it that we want our world to be? As God's children, we're heirs to the kingdom and the kingdom is all that there is. All the abundance God has is right there for us as we continue to be transformed by the renewing of our minds. The Christ in us is asking to come forth, to be what it is we've asked to be.

We all need to take some time this week just to love ourselves completely, regardless of who we are or what's going on — put all that love on us. And then watch how the spirit just moves and we become a magnet of love that draws all things to us. Divine Love always will, and always has, supplied all of our needs. Begin to see that Divine Love is working in and through everything.

As we begin to say Divine Love will supply our needs, we have to remember the power of the spoken word. As we are transformed, our words are transformed. We stop using "can't." We stop using "don't have." We stop using those words that negate the abundance God has given us.

The words we speak bring life or death into our lives. We want life, abundance, joy, peace, and harmony in who we are. We want those things in our lives, and in the lives of the people around us. We have to remember that in every apparent challenge or situation we're being transformed and that our minds are being renewed because we're staying in the Christ Consciousness, which means we're keeping our consciousness on God and only God.

I would like to end this book with a prayer and a positive affirmation:

Heavenly Mother-Father God, we thank you right now for your spirit touching the person who reads this book. You said you would open the door that man could not close and we come knowing that you are within our midst. We thank you for this power flowing in and through each one of us, touching us in a special way, lifting us up and releasing us from those parts of ourselves that have created illusions of lack and limitation in our lives.

We thank you for touching our minds in a special way, releasing us from all the pain, anguish, and resentment that have brought illusions into our lives. Heal us, so that right here and right now we are transformed. We have been renewed, so that truly the Christ Consciousness in us comes forth boldly, with courage, stepping forth and being what you would have us to be.

We thank you for touching our children in a special way. We thank you because we know that the doors have already been opened. We thank you for giving them the courage to walk through them, for lettering their angels, their guides and their teachers work with them. We thank you right here and right now for your power, for your peace, for your joy, and your love which flows through us; and that wherever we go, we are supernaturally blessed and well-favored, and people cannot resist helping us or helping our children, opening doors or teaching them things.

We thank you right here and right now for your peace and your love that will always follow us, surround us and proceed us in every aspect of our lives. And so it is.

Peace and love, light and joy
        Sesvalah

Be sure to pick up the accompanying journal

Speaking it into Existence *Everyday*

Sesvalah

with Naleighna Kai

Macro Publishing Group

ISBN: 0-9702699-7-8

www.macropublishing.com

available online at
www.amazon.com

My Joy is the Journey

Deirdre J. Burrell, DD, LAc, CVT, Metaphysician

ISBN: 09778734-5-5

Journal:

www.deirdrejburell.com

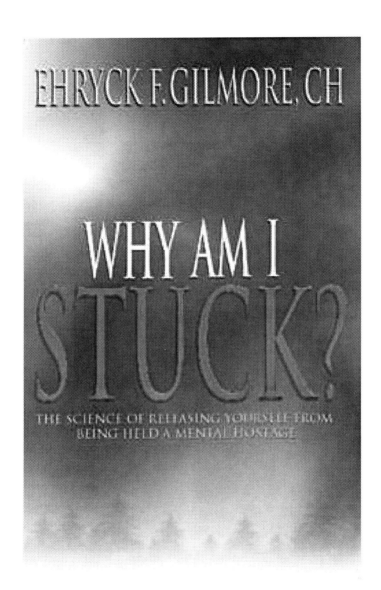

EHRYCK F. GILMORE, CH

WHY AM I STUCK?

THE SCIENCE OF RELEASING YOURSELF FROM
BEING HELD A MENTAL HOSTAGE

ISBN: 0-9759120-0-3

Jounral ISBN: 0-9759120-1-1

www.whyamistuck.com

books by J. L. Woodson

ISBN: 0-9754130-0-7

ISBN: 1-59309-059-5

ISBN: 1-593090218

"Writing with a finesse beyond his years, Woodson blends humor, reality and survival. He creates an inspiring story told with the innocent candor that can only exist when belief in humanity is still fresh."
—*RAWSISTAZ Book Club*

www.jlwoodson.com

Naleighna Kai, (pronounced Na-Lay-na Ki), is a Chicago native and the author of *Every Woman Needs a Wife* (Strebor Books/ Simon & Schuster) and the coauthor of *How to Win the Publishing Game.* *She* writes fiction, romance, erotica, New Thought, and science fiction.

Her next novel, *She Touched My Soul,* will be released in January 2007. She works for a major law firm in Chicago and is currently working on her next projects: *Open Door Marriage, Was it Good for You, Too?* and *Right Place, Right Time.*

visit her on the web:
www.naleighnakai.com
naleighna@naleighnakai.com

Sesvalah,
M.S.W., L.C.S.W,

(pronounced Says-va-lah), is a former program director for a Chicago social service agency, a licensed clinical social worker, sexual and child abuse counselor and a family therapist. She is also the founding pastor of a teaching and healing center in Chicago. She has served as a speaker, moderator and panelist for sexual abuse and domestic violence symposiums nationwide.

Her book, *Speak it into Existence,* skillfully weaves insightful observations with heartwarming, humorous and uplifting stories along with useful guides and tools for achieving harmonious relationships to healing from stressful and abusive situations, and changing thought processes on life. This book expands on the belief that "If you change the way you *think*, you'll change the way you *live*."

Sesvalah has a private therapy practice in Chicago and is the mother of two children. She resides in Harvey, Illinois with her family where she is working on her next book, *As Clear as a Bell.*

Sesvalah is available for speaking engagements, domestic violence or child abuse symposiums, as well as book signings.

sesvalah@macropublishing.com
www.sesvalah.com

CPSIA information can be obtained at www.ICGtesting.com
Printed in the USA
LVOW040534260912

300369LV00001B/51/A